TYING
BETTER
FLIES

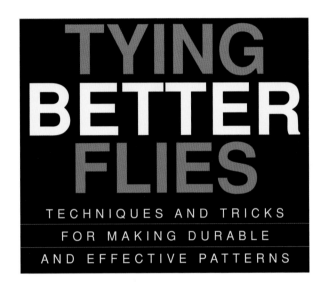

TYING BETTER FLIES

TECHNIQUES AND TRICKS FOR MAKING DURABLE AND EFFECTIVE PATTERNS

ART SCHECK

The Countryman Press

Woodstock, Vermont

Library of Congress Cataloging-in-Publication Data
Scheck, Art.
    Tying better flies : techniques and tricks for making durable and effective patterns / Art Scheck.—1st ed.
    p. cm.
    ISBN 0-88150-583-8
    1. Fly tying. I. Title.
SH451.S314 2003
688.7'9124—dc21

                                        2003048591

Cover and interior design by Carol Jessop, Black Trout Design
Cover and interior photographs by Art Scheck

Published by The Countryman Press, P.O. Box 748, Woodstock, VT 05091

Distributed by W. W. Norton & Company, Inc., 500 Fifth Avenue, New York NY 10110

Printed in Belgium

10 9 8 7 6 5 4 3 2 1

CONTENTS

ACKNOWLEDGMENTS

It's hard to know where to begin—or stop. As an angling editor and writer, I've had the benefit of conversations and correspondence with some of the world's best fly tiers. A number of people stand out as having been particularly helpful and generous over the years: John Betts, Ed Engle, Ted Fauceglia, Jay Fullum, Chris Helm, Dave Hughes, Ed Jaworowski, Dave Klausmeyer, Jim Krul, Bill Merg, Skip Morris, Rich Osthoff, Boyd Pfeiffer, John Shewey, Dick Talleur, Bill Tapply, Gordon Wickstrom, and Davy Wotton. My thanks to them and all the other tiers who have furthered my education.

My wife, Mary Jo, has endured my fly-tying habit and its attendant clutter since 1988, and to her I owe special thanks. No woman should have to watch her daughters leave for school with tufts of marabou and bits of tinsel stuck to their shoelaces, or come home from work to find her dining-room table covered by an army of still-sticky epoxy flies, or discover strange stains on the countertops left as results of mishaps with dyes, or need to remember *never* to enter her husband's office barefoot lest she step on one of the 80 size 18 dry-fly hooks permanently stuck in the rug, but my woman has put up with all that and worse. I could not pursue this delightful madness without her.

My main purpose in this book is to share some techniques and tricks that will help you tie better flies. Perhaps I should explain what I mean by "better." I don't claim that the flies in this book will always catch more and bigger fish than other flies will, though all of them will catch plenty of fish. Nor do I claim that the types of flies described herein are always more exact and realistic replicas of fish food than other types are, though they look enough like food to dupe lots of gamefish and panfish. My emphasis is on *how* to tie flies; on techniques, components, and little tricks that produce fake insects and ersatz minnows that act as you want them to and stay in one piece; on construction methods that solve problems and yield practical fishing lures. For "better," then, you can read "practical, predictable, consistent, durable, and versatile."

All my life, I've enjoyed taking things apart and putting things together. Give me a new, expensive fly reel—or, better yet, a levelwind reel with three zillion tiny parts—and my hands start itching to disassemble it. I get a genuine happiness from using tools and making parts fit. Some people approach fly tying as artists; others come at it as naturalists or philosophers. I approach fly tying as a mechanic.

Patterns matter, of course, but construction interests me more. Some combinations of materials and colors and proportions—fly *patterns,* in other words—catch fish very well, but only in certain places or at specific times. A good construction—that is, a good method of assembling parts—can be endlessly modified to become any number of patterns. The patterns that have worked for me might not work as well for you; your fish might prefer flies made in other colors and sizes. You have to figure out those details for yourself. But construction methods that work for me will certainly work just as well for you.

One of the headaches of writing a fly-tying book is deciding what to include and what to leave out. This book doesn't pretend to be a comprehensive, exhaustive treatment of fly-tying techniques. Rather, it covers a dozen or so major concepts or designs that I think will prove useful to every freshwater fly fisher and many saltwater anglers. Some chapters address problems that frustrate many tiers—making the head of a Muddler or the hackle of a parachute fly, for instance. Others deal with ways to achieve neatness and durability—how to dub a nymph, reinforce a palmered hackle, build a three-layer wing on a bucktail, or create a dry fly's upright wings. Still other sections teach simple, inexpensive, and commonsensical designs—tiny flies that don't have many parts, extra-buoyant caddis and mayfly designs that don't require hackle feathers, and baitfish flies that don't get snagged. Novice and journeymen tiers in particular should find the techniques in this book helpful, but even veterans might pick up a few tricks.

Every type of fly in this book can be tied to represent many species of fish food. While you might not learn 200 different mayfly patterns, you will learn reliable, durable constructions that imitate mayfly duns and emergers, caddisfly adults, caddis pupae, mayfly nymphs, stonefly nymphs, and various types of baitfish. That's a pretty good assortment of lures. And, more important, you will acquire essential skills that let you tie all sorts of flies. You will become a better fly mechanic—and that can only result in tying better flies.

A few years before he passed away, the great outdoor writer H. G. "Tap" Tapply gave me a copy of a little book that he wrote in 1939. It's called *The Fly Tyer's Handbook,* and it deals with the construction of various types of flies. In the letter that he tucked inside the cover, Tap explained why he'd written the book. When he first became interested in fly tying,

Tap said, he'd been frustrated by books that "told me what to do but not how to do it." So he went to his employer, National Sportsman Inc., with a plan for "a simple little booklet telling *how* to tie flies." Tap's idea became a 72-page book published by National Sportsman in 1940. A more elegant, hardcover second edition was brought out in 1949 by Tap's friend Oliver Durrell and, Tap said, "sold quite briskly."

I can only hope that this book will have the staying power of Tap Tapply's *Fly Tyer's Handbook.* But the intent is the same: to tell *how* to tie flies.

In the introduction to his little book, Tap expressed his chief wish for his readers: ". . . [A]fter he has learned the mechanics of fly tying, he can lay this book aside and carry on under his own power, so to speak." I like that phrase: "the mechanics of fly tying." And I hope that you find this book helpful in learning some of them.

Art Scheck
March 2003

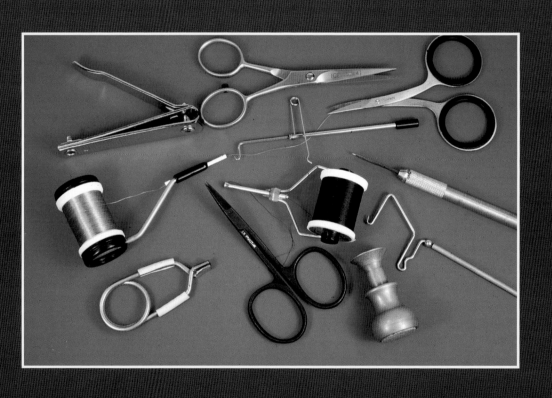

A fly tier could spend an astonishing lot of money on tools. Some do, perhaps figuring that the prospect of an inheritance only makes one's heirs soft and shiftless, and that money serves a higher end if it purchases an array of top-shelf fly-tying tools and gadgets. There's no denying the pleasure that comes from handling and using fine tools or the frustration that results from trying to do good work with shoddily made implements.

Having reliable tools and enough of them makes a difference. For most of its practitioners, though, fly tying remains a low-tech craft. An amateur who wants only to keep his fly boxes filled with sturdy, versatile, effective patterns can do first-rate work with a small kit of midpriced tools. I have an absurd number of fly-tying tools and gadgets, some of them purchased over the past 30-odd years and some given to me during my years as an editor and writer. But all the tools I really *need* to tie good flies—indeed, all the tools I regularly use—fit in a small shoe box with room to spare. None of my workhorse tools is the most expensive of its kind. As time goes by, I find myself using fewer tools rather than more.

The purpose of this chapter is not to present a comprehensive overview of all fly-tying tools, but simply to share a few thoughts on those needed to tie the flies in this book. It's not a very long list.

VISES

The standard advice goes something like, "Buy the best vise you can afford." That made perfect sense years ago, when fly tiers had only a few models from which to choose. I tied my first flies with a cheap, flimsy, pot-metal contraption that came with my mother's kit. It didn't hold hooks of any size or shape well, and its soft jaws quickly deformed. When Mom got a better vise—the one that's on the cover of this book—our fly tying instantly became easier and less frustrating. Back then, in the late 1960s, the choice was between a cheap, pot-metal clamp that never worked and one of the handful of reasonably good vises on the market.

These days, tiers can choose among many vises, and getting a good one doesn't have to mean buying the most expensive model in the shop. A top-of-the-line Renzetti vise is a marvel of the machinist's art and a pleasure to contemplate and handle, and no one who buys such a tool ever regrets the purchase. But even Renzetti's entry-level vise is a fine tool that's better than anything available when I was a kid. Griffin Enterprises makes some fancy vises loaded with accessories and features—but Griffin's simplest, least costly model will squeeze a hook hard enough to make it whimper. Nowadays, the choice is

A vise usually has a "sweet spot" in the jaws where it holds a hook most easily. High-quality vises typically have larger sweet spots than cheap vises have. When you put a hook in your vise, place it so that the jaws close on the lower part of the bend. Do not bury the point of the hook within the jaws, and do not use the very tips of the jaws to grab only a tiny portion of the hook.

not between worthless and adequate, but among good, better, *really* good, and amazing. Even a fly tier on a budget can have a very good vise.

The marketplace also contains some junk, of course, some of which costs only a little less than an entry-level vise from a respected manufacturer. This is one case in which it pays to look for certain brand names. Regal, Renzetti, Dyna-King, D. H. Thompson, Griffin, and HMH are among the names to look for. Fellow fly tiers can steer you toward trustworthy tools from other companies.

Vises employ various mechanisms to close their jaws and hold a hook. Some have cams that push or pull the jaws into a collet. Others use thumbscrews to adjust and close their jaws. Still others have combinations of adjustment screws and cams. Regal vises have spring-loaded jaws; squeezing a lever opens the jaws, and releasing the lever lets the vise close to grab the hook. All of these systems work well, and you don't have to worry about differences among basic designs. Vises are like other tools: After you use one for a while, you become comfortable with it, and then other tools seem awkward.

My own requirements are pretty simple. Mostly, I want a vise to handle a wide range of hooks and to hold them very securely. Besides tying fresh- and saltwater flies, I also make spinnerbaits and buzzbaits. Sometimes I need a tool that will hold a very small dry-fly hook; other times, I need something that will hold a size 4/0 spinnerbait hook while I sharpen the point with a file. This is perhaps a larger range of sizes than a typical freshwater fly tier deals with.

I prefer a vise that has an adjustable head. When I tie small flies, I often tilt the head upward to provide more working room at the back end of a tiny hook. When I tie Clouser Deep Minnows, I move the head downward until it's nearly horizontal; that makes it easier to invert the hook after attaching the belly hair. With most other flies, I leave the head at about a 45-degree angle.

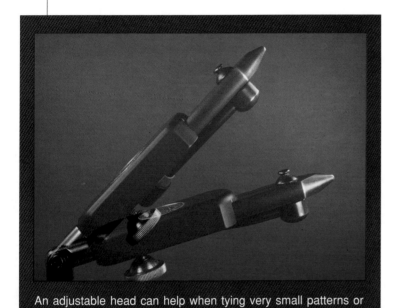

An adjustable head can help when tying very small patterns or upside-down flies such as Clouser Minnows. Tilting the head up provides a little more working room at the stern of a tiny hook.

Those are my only functional requirements, though I do have one other need. I shoot a fair number of fly-tying photos. When possible, I shoot them with a ring flash attached to the camera, and often with a small booster flash. Strobe photography is quicker and more comfortable than shooting under my big photoflood lamps, which generate a frightening amount of heat. But even in the hands of an expert (which I ain't), a flash can produce "hot spots" in a photo—areas where reflective surfaces show up as, well, flashes of white light. That's why most of my step-by-step images show my Regal vise: It has no flat, shiny surfaces that can reflect light and spoil a photo.

I also like the Regal because it's fast and easy to operate. That matters when I take pictures because I often use two vises. I learned long ago not to try tying a fly while reaching over and around a camera. Try building a fly while standing, with the vise at an inconvenient height and at arm's length, and with an obstruction four inches away from the vise, and you'll see what I mean. When I shoot a simple step-by-step sequence, my Regal sits in front of the camera and holds the fly for each photo. I construct each stage of the fly on the other side of the table, where I can sit down and use my Griffin Patriot vise. This procedure entails a lot of movement, but it lets me get the results I want (eventually, anyway). The Regal's squeeze-and-release operation makes the process a little easier.

So, that's why you see a Regal vise in all the step-by-step photos in this book. I'm not on Regal's payroll; nor do I dislike tools made by other companies. Yes, the Regal is an excellent vise that I'd be glad to have whether or not I took photos. But since I do take fly-tying pictures, my Regal vise shows up in most of them.

The other vise I use a lot is one of the early Griffin Patriots, which Bernie Griffin sent to me shortly after he brought out the design. This, too, is a first-rate vise, though its massive, blunt jaws can complicate tying a size 20 or smaller fly. It's not that the Patriot is unsuitable for tying tiny flies; but it's just not ideal for making midges. On the other hand, it will hold any hook up to about size 7/0 (maybe larger; I've never tried) with rock-solid security. It's a good example of high quality without a high price tag.

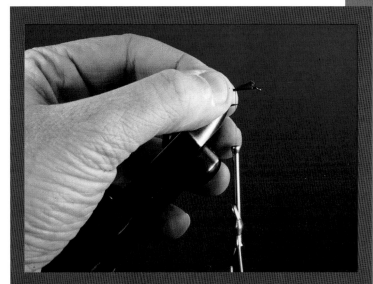

Some aspects of tool selection are entirely personal. I hold the vise a lot while I tie, and so I prefer one with a wide, flat head that makes a comfortable rest for my left hand.

Both the Regal and the Patriot have relatively wide heads, and I like that. I rest my left hand on the vise while holding a component in place, and a broad, flat head is more comfortable than a narrow, rounded one. That's the sort of personal preference that can figure into a buying decision.

The heads of my Patriot and Regal rotate, though neither is a genuine rotary vise in the way that a Renzetti is. With a Renzetti (and some other vises), the shank of the hook is the axis of rotation. When the tier rotates the vise, the fly turns without changing its angle or moving up and down. That's a nifty feature that, among other things, lets a tier apply a material by spinning the hook. Rotating the head of my Regal or Patriot, on the other hand, changes the attitude of the fly. I can turn the head to inspect the far side of a fly or get a better angle to attach a particular component, but I can't do any truly rotary tying.

Does that matter? Is a fly tier better off with, to borrow Renzetti's advertising slogan, a "true rotary" vise? Many tiers would say yes. Certainly, there's no disadvantage to having such a vise. I've used a few of Renzetti's vises and I like them very much. But I'm a creature of habit who tends to keep using whatever tools he has until they wear out. I can say that I've never met anyone who regretted owning a true rotary vise.

Although vises differ greatly in design, operation, and features, any of the good ones will let you tie excellent flies. A few are better suited to jumbo hooks; a few are better with small hooks; the vast majority work well enough with any hook a fly fisher is likely to use. Some tiers love to have lots of accessories—a materials clip, an offset mount for the head, an adjustment for rotational resistance, interchangeable jaws, a bobbin rest or cradle, a gallows tool for tying parachute flies. Other guys take the bare-bones approach; neither of my vises has so much as a materials clip. Both attitudes seem equally valid to me. And remember that it's okay to buy a vise simply because you *like* it.

Pedestal base or C-clamp? I'd recommend getting both. A pedestal base lets you tie anywhere—at a friend's house, at a club meeting, in a motel room. A C-clamp base provides perfect stability at your permanent work area and brings the vise head a few inches closer to you than a pedestal does. Some vises come with both; most companies supply one type of base with a vise and sell the other separately. Most vises have ⅜-inch shafts, which means that they'll work not only with their own bases or clamps, but with at least some of those made by other companies as well.

SCISSORS

Every fly has materials that need to be cut or trimmed, and that alone makes good scissors a worthwhile investment. You'll need at least two pairs: one with short blades and fine tips for detail work, and a larger, more robust pair for cutting and trimming clumps of hair. Most fly tiers end up with more than that; I generally have four or five pairs of scissors on my bench.

When you shop for heavy scissors, look for those that have fine serrations on one blade. The serrations let the blades hold on to a clump of material, which makes for easier, more precise cutting. Fine scissors for detail work can have plain blades or one serrated blade; even when trimming a single fiber, though, you will find that a blade with fine serrations makes a difference.

Although they're expensive, top-of-the-line scissors last long enough to justify their cost. No other fly-tying tool endures as much constant wear and tear. But not everyone can or wants to spend, say, $150 on two pairs of scissors. You can greatly extend the life of inexpensive scissors by buying three pairs—one fine and two heavy—and using each for specific jobs. Restrict the fine-tipped scissors to small work: snipping the thread, clipping a few hackle fibers, and similar tasks. Use one of the heavier pairs for cutting or trimming components on a fly: tail and wing butts, the tag end of a tinsel rib, the excess portion of a

It's possible, albeit difficult, to tie flies without a vise, bobbin, or whip-finish tool. People did so for centuries. Scissors, however, are indispensable. A fly tier needs at least two pairs—a small, fine-tipped pair for detail work, and a heavier pair for cutting clumps of hair and other bulky or coarse materials. Good scissors, such as the German pair in the middle, justify their cost by their longevity.

nymph's wing case, and so on. Save the other heavy pair for chopping clumps of hair from bucktails or calf tails, cutting pieces of oval tinsel, and suchlike chores. By splitting up the workload this way, you won't inflict too much wear on any single tool.

Don't cut wire, heavy oval tinsel, or even monofilament with your scissors. Use toenail clippers for those jobs.

Make sure that the finger holes are large enough to accommodate your thumb and forefinger. Some of the surgical scissors sold by fly-tying suppliers have tiny finger holes barely large enough to fit a small woman's hands. A man with average hands would find such tools difficult and uncomfortable to use; a guy with big mitts might find them useless.

Be very careful about resharpening scissors. It's a job best left to a professional. I have a very old pair of Thompson's original Ice Scissors that I've resharpened a couple of times (they've cut and trimmed the parts of at least 50,000 flies), and while they still work pretty well, they're not as sharp as they originally were. The sharpening services offered by some fly shops are well worth paying for.

THREAD BOBBINS

Bobbins come in many sizes and styles. Some fly tiers develop a fanatical loyalty to one type, but others, including me, take a more catholic view. Indeed, I don't see any functional differences among the various designs. The tool's jobs are to hold the spool of thread, protect the thread from abrasion by keeping it away from the tier's fingertips, and permit the accurate placement of each wrap. All bobbins accomplish those things.

But I do care about materials. A plain metal tube can develop grooves or burrs that cut the thread, rendering the tool useless and causing profanity. Ceramic tubes or metal tubes with ceramic tips will last indefinitely. It's worth spending a few extra bucks on a bobbin that has a ceramic tube or insert. Buy two of them, or even three. I sometimes have four bobbins on my bench, each loaded with a different color or type of thread.

Fly shops offer all sorts of handy gadgets for threading bobbins. Many tiers, including me, use dental-floss threaders or homemade tools fashioned from very fine wire.

Most fly-tying thread is prewaxed. Some of the wax rubs off on the inside of the bobbin tube, where it can build up and eventually clog the tube. Light threads hardly ever cause this problem, but some middleweight and heavy threads, particularly size 3/0 Monocord, can quickly leave a lot of wax inside a bobbin tube. If your bobbin's tube becomes plugged with wax, clean it with a piece of fly-line backing. Thread about 4 inches of 20-pound Dacron through your bobbin threader, and pull the doubled backing through the tube from top to bottom. The backing will scrub the inside of the tube clean.

When you need to pull very hard on the thread, such as when spinning deer hair, hold the bobbin so that the tube points more or less at the hook. Try to avoid putting a heavy sideways load on the tube; you could damage or break the tool.

WHIP-FINISH TOOLS

Every fly tier should learn to make the whip finish by hand, but a tool is still a handy thing, if only because it eliminates the chance of abrading the thread with rough fingers. Back when I lived in New England and split a fair amount of kindling, my hands became a mess every winter. I couldn't tie a whip finish by hand because my rough, cracked fingers ruined the thread.

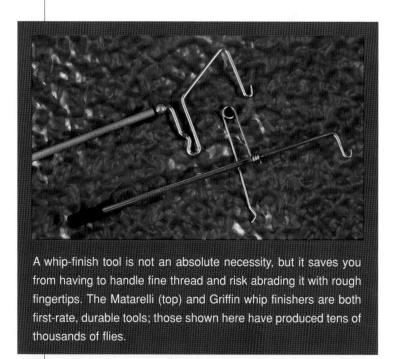

A whip-finish tool is not an absolute necessity, but it saves you from having to handle fine thread and risk abrading it with rough fingertips. The Matarelli (top) and Griffin whip finishers are both first-rate, durable tools; those shown here have produced tens of thousands of flies.

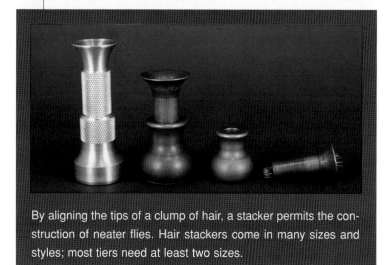

By aligning the tips of a clump of hair, a stacker permits the construction of neater flies. Hair stackers come in many sizes and styles; most tiers need at least two sizes.

For my money, the Matarelli whip-finish tool remains the best. Griffin also makes an excellent, easy-to-use whip finisher, as do a few other outfits.

Beginning tiers have trouble with the whip-finish knot because they try to make it with the thread as taut as a guitar string. Once you've mounted the tool on the thread (or the thread on the tool, depending on your point of view), you don't need much more thread tension than the weight of the bobbin supplies.

HAIR STACKERS

I don't know where these tools originally came from, but I can't remember seeing any when my mother was teaching me to tie flies in the 1960s. I've heard of guys using spent pistol cartridges to stack hair; maybe that's where the idea originated. These days, hair stackers come in dozens of sizes and shapes, but they all do the same thing: align the tips of all the hairs in a clump. Some flies are nearly impossible to tie well without a hair stacker; others simply look neater with stacked wings or tails.

Unless you tie a very limited range of flies, you'll want at least two stackers: a tiny one for making the wings of small dry flies, and a medium-size one for other jobs. If you tie a broad variety of flies, you will probably end up with three or four hair stackers of various sizes.

I like brass stackers better than aluminum ones, though I'm not willing to fight about it. A broad base keeps a stacker from tipping over, and a felt, rubber, or cork pad keeps it from denting the furniture. A flared tube makes inserting a clump of hair easier.

There's no need to bang a hair stacker hard enough to drive a nail. Tapping it several times on your desk will usually align all the hairs in the tube.

HACKLE PLIERS

Like other tools, hackle pliers come in a variety of designs. Old-fashioned, English-style hackle pliers probably remain the most popular type, and there's little need for anything more complicated. All we require of these tools is that they hold feathers securely and without breaking the stems.

The important differences among hackle pliers lie not in design but in quality. Cheap pliers imported from a developing country are likely to have jaws with sharp edges or burrs that can cut hackle stems. Low-quality hackle pliers might also have uneven jaws that don't grip a feather well. Even with so simple a tool as this, it pays to spend three or four dollars more and get pliers with nicely made jaws.

If your hackle pliers seem to break a lot of feathers, look for burrs or sharp edges on the jaws. You can polish off such defects with extra-fine emery paper or, more easily, a high-speed rotary tool (such as a Dremel) equipped with a sanding disk. Another way to solve the stem-cutting problem while also improving the pliers' grip is to force a piece of vinyl tubing over each jaw. Shops that sell aquarium supplies carry such tubing in a variety of sizes. My workhorse pliers have pieces of vinyl tubing on their jaws, and they never break hackle feathers.

I added another modification to one pair of English-style hackle pliers that makes the tool more comfortable to use. Opening these particular pliers requires a vigorous squeeze. They hold a feather very well, but squeezing them hard enough to spread the jaws was almost painful. So, I stripped an inch of insulation off heavy electrical wire, split the insulation lengthwise with a razor blade, and used Super Glue to attach one piece of split insulation to each side of the tool. The insulation has no value as a cushion, but it does widen the areas on which I push.

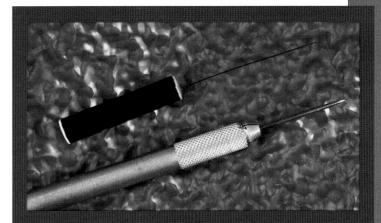

Pieces of clear vinyl tubing make good pads on the jaws of English-style hackle pliers. These pliers also have a pad made of wire insulation superglued to each side, making them more comfortable to operate.

A needle vise (bottom) makes a good bodkin. For applying head cement or lacquer, I use a homemade tool consisting of a piece of fine wire epoxied into a short length of dowel.

BODKINS

A pin vise makes an excellent bodkin, and it has the advantage of having a heavy-duty, replaceable needle. My pin vise can also hold a 1/16-inch drill bit, which comes in handy when I want to makes holes for rubber legs in balsa or cork popper bodies.

I reserve my pin-vise bodkin for jobs that require a needle—picking out fur to make legs on a nymph, splitting a section from a cemented goose quill to make a wing case, dividing a clump of hair to make dry-fly wings, and so forth. Most fly tiers also use bodkins to apply head cement, but I don't. For one thing, using a bodkin as a cement applicator means that I have to wipe off the tool after each fly or scrape off a crust of dried cement when I want to use the needle. More important, a needle can pick up a fairly large drop of cement or lacquer, often more than a small trout fly requires. For applying head cement, I use a homemade tool consisting of a piece of No. 3 or No. 4 stainless leader wire mounted in a piece of dowel. The thin wire lets me pick up a tiny droplet of cement and apply it very precisely.

MISCELLANEOUS TOOLS AND GADGETS

Small, smooth-jawed, duckbill pliers are good tools for flattening the barbs of most hooks. And please flatten all your barbs, not only to lessen the chance of injuring fish that you want to release, but also because accidents happen. Even a small hook can put a big dent in your fun if it ends up stuck in the connective tissue of a knuckle. Some years ago, a friend and I

Smooth-jawed duckbill pliers work well for flattening barbs. Small needle-nose pliers come in handy on any workbench. Fine tweezers simplify picking up small hooks.

ran across a young chap who had buried one of a crankbait's hooks in a tendon. It was a small lure with small trebles, probably size 12, but we couldn't get that one little hook out of the poor guy's finger. His day of smallmouth fishing turned into a trip to the emergency room. Had the hook been barbless, a Band-Aid and a little cursing would have taken care of the mishap.

While you're at the hardware store, also pick up a pair of small needle-nosed pliers. They have many uses on any workbench. Get fine-tipped tweezers, too; they come in handy for picking up small hooks.

These days, most fly-tying hooks have excellent points. The chemically sharpened points of premium hooks are frighteningly keen right out of the box. But some of the older hook designs have cut or ground points that often require sharpening, particularly in larger sizes. Tackle shops sell a variety of hook-sharpening gadgets, but I do all my at-home sharpening with small and medium-size triangular files. The hardware trade calls them slim taper files. Don't waste money on cheap files; look for the Nicholson brand. You should also carry a small hook sharpener in your vest or tackle bag in case you need to touch up a point in the field.

Film canisters make good containers for dubbing blends and other materials. If you don't shoot 35-millimeter or Advanced Photo System film, you can probably pick up all the empty canisters you want at the nearest photo lab.

A small brush with short, stiff bristles is a fine tool for fuzzing up the dubbed body of a wet fly or nymph. The steel dubbing teasers sold in fly shops accomplish the same thing, but their razor-sharp barbs can cut the thread beneath the dubbing and might even damage a fly's rib. Plastic bristles won't hurt your flies. A cheap toothbrush with the bristles trimmed short (use sturdy scissors or shears to trim them) works well enough. A .22-caliber bore-cleaning brush also makes a good dubbing teaser, though it's not so gentle as a plastic brush.

A small comb, such as an eyebrow or mustache comb, does a good job of removing fuzz and broken fibers from a clump of deer hair, calf tail, woodchuck hair, and so forth.

You can find these tools in any drugstore. I've long used a Maybelline eyebrow gadget that has a fine comb on one side and a brush on the other. With the brush's bristles trimmed short, the tool serves as both a hair cleaner and a dubbing teaser.

Many fly tiers, particularly those who tie bass bugs, use double-edged razor blades to trim deer hair. I often use a double-edged blade to rough out the shape of a Muddler's head, though I finish shaping the hair with scissors. A single-edged razor comes in handy for scraping a botched, half-completed fly off a hook. This happens to everyone, by the way. When a fly starts to go terribly wrong, don't waste time trying to untie the thing. Snip the thread and hack all the materials off the hook with a single-edged razor.

A well-stocked fly shop offers dozens of other fly-tying gadgets. Some, such as dubbing-loop twisters, are valuable, useful tools, though they're not required for tying the flies in this book. Certain other tools strike me as gadgetry for the sake of gadgetry. They might indeed work as advertised, but they don't solve any problems that can't be solved with the 10 original tools attached to your hands. Not that there's anything wrong with gadgetry for its own sake.

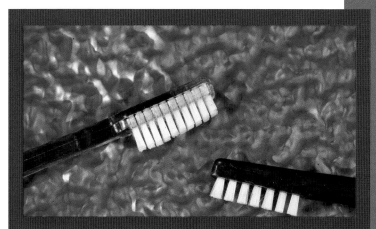

Plastic brushes with short, stiff bristles are good dubbing teasers that won't damage any of a fly's components. A cheap toothbrush with the bristles cut short works fine for this purpose.

Like any normal American guy, I own all sorts of tools that I hardly ever use. My wife knows better than to leave me unsupervised in a Sears, auto-parts, or hardware store. But tying better flies requires a fairly small assortment of tools, none of which needs to be the most expensive example of its kind.

We'll look at specific materials as we tackle each type of fly. Every fly, however, requires a hook and thread, and most flies call for some type of cement or finish. So, it makes sense to devote a short chapter to these items.

You will notice that while I mention quite a few products by name—a Mustad hook, for instance, or a Danville thread—I rarely recommend a particular brand or model. That's not because I'm lazy or because I don't know the differences among various products. Rather, it's because I believe that many fly-tying products are interchangeable with others. It simply doesn't matter that one tier prefers 8/0 Uni-Thread while another likes Flymaster 6/0; neither will catch more trout because of his taste in thread. Tiemco TMC 3761 and a Mustad 3906B hooks are not identical, but they're similar enough for our purposes, and a nymph tied on one is no better or worse than a nymph tied on the other. And fish don't care whether a fly tier seals the heads of his flies with homemade flexible cement or imported British lacquer. One of my goals in writing this chapter is to help a beginning or journeyman tier relax when he shops for hooks, thread, or cement.

HOOKS

The hook industry does not have universal and exact standards. There is no International Society of Fish-Hook Engineers that has established the gap of a size 12 hook as precisely something-point-something millimeters. One company's size 12 hook might be (and probably is) a smidgen larger or smaller than another company's size 12.

With most trout-fly hooks, the difference is usually just that—a smidgen. If you read a recipe that calls for a standard, size 14 dry-fly hook, don't worry about the differences among brands. Use whatever brand of hook you have, or buy whatever the local shop carries. Then tie the fly and go catch a fish.

With saltwater, bass-bug, and salmon-fly hooks, the differences among competitive models become more pronounced. If a fly-tying author believes that the exact dimensions of the hook matter when tying a particular pattern, then he should specify a manufacturer and model as well as a size. Fortunately, though, many warmwater and saltwater patterns work well on a variety of frames.

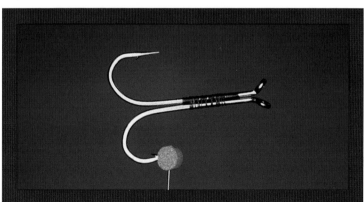

The information on a package of hooks is a description, not a set of specifications. Both of these hooks are size 8, 2X-long nymph models. As you can see, they differ slightly in gap, shape, and length. The maker of the top hook describes it as being made of "heavy" wire; the bottom hook, according to its manufacturer, is made of "standard" wire. There's no practical difference between the two wires. Learn to pick hooks according to how well they suit your purposes, and regard the descriptions on labels as, at best, rough guides.

"Size" usually refers to the dimension of a hook's gap. Each manufacturer might have its own size scale, but the marketplace prevents a company from using a scale that differs drastically from those of its competitors. If the nominally size 12 nymph hooks made by the Super-Pointy Hook Company were equivalent to every other company's size 18 hooks, Super-Pointy wouldn't make many sales—or at least many repeat sales.

Things become a bit muddier when we start talking about shank length and wire diameter. A nymph recipe might call for a 2X-long hook. That term is a description, not a specification. On paper, a 2X-long hook has a shank equal in length to that of a standard hook two sizes larger. But what is the "standard" used as the basis of comparison? It varies from manufacturer to manufacturer, and even from one family of hooks to another in the same company's catalog. And what does "two sizes" mean? The answer to that, too, can differ from company to company. One manufacturer might say that 10 is two sizes larger than 14. Another might contend that 12 is two sizes larger than 14, arguing that size 13 exists, even if the company doesn't use it. So, hooks with nominally identical descriptions—size 12, 2X long—can differ slightly in actual length.

Likewise, terms such as "2X-heavy wire" refer to unidentified standards. One manufacturer, eager to tout the strength of its steel, might designate as standard the wire it uses for dry-fly hooks. At this company, a garden-variety nymph hook might have a 2X-heavy designation. A competitor might use wire exactly as thick for its nymph hooks, but call it standard, making this outfit's dry-fly hooks 2X light, even though they're virtually identical to the "standard weight" hooks made by the first company.

Things get stranger. Over the years, a few hook-company executives have admitted to me that sometimes they simply fudge the specs, calling a new hook 3X long and 2X heavy because that's how competitors describe similar models. Furthermore, very few hook companies make their own wire. Most buy wire, and they can't always get the stuff in perfect size increments. A given series of hooks might have a disproportionate jump in wire diameter between two sizes because the ideal wire—the one the hook designer wanted—simply isn't available.

And so on, until thinking about hooks makes your head explode. So, relax. Follow the lead of the politically correct and learn to celebrate diversity. If the industry had precise, universal standards, we wouldn't have such a large variety of subtly different hook models available to us. Fish food doesn't come in perfectly graduated sizes that correspond exactly to the sizes of hooks, and sometimes it helps to have three slightly different size 14 dry-fly hooks.

Think of the hook as a fly's frame or chassis. Worry less about descriptions such as 2X long or 1X fine, and more about how well a particular hook will work as the chassis of the bug, minnow, or crustacean that you want to build. Learn to think, "That's a good frame for

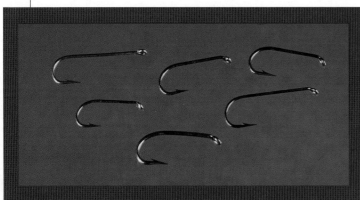

Dry-fly hooks come in various shapes and lengths, but they're all made of relatively thin wire. Compare the standard wet-fly hook at the bottom of the picture to the five dry-fly models above it. The Aberdeen bait hook (top, left) is a good, inexpensive long-shank hook for dry flies.

an imitation of one of those little tan caddis-flies I saw yesterday," or, "That's about the right length and weight for a black stonefly nymph." Ideally, you should be able to pick the right hook out of a box containing dozens of different sizes and styles, none of them labeled. With time and experience, you will develop this ability. Think first about the general type of hook you want, and then pay attention to differences among models.

Freshwater fly hooks, or at least most of them, can be divided into several categories. Dry flies require hooks made of relatively light wire; compared to a wet-fly hook the same size, a dry-fly hook is made of thinner steel. A standard, traditional dry-fly hook has a shank roughly twice as long as the gap is deep. Its bend is more or less round. Besides traditional models, most companies also offer long-shank dry-fly hooks, which are useful for tying hoppers, crickets, some mayflies, and floating stone-flies. Light-wire Aberdeen bait hooks, though rarely used by fly tiers, are excellent long-shank hooks for dry flies; I've caught a lot of fish on dry flies tied on inexpensive Mustad 3261 Aberdeen hooks.

A traditional wet-fly hook is generally a tad shorter in the shank than a dry-fly hook the same nominal size. It's made of much heavier wire, and it probably has a decreasing-radius Sproat bend.

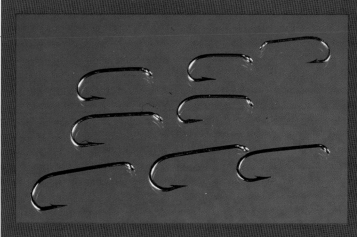

Wet-fly and nymph hooks are made of heavier wire than those used for floating flies. The hook at the upper right-hand corner is a dry-fly model included for the sake of comparison; the other seven are for wets or nymphs.

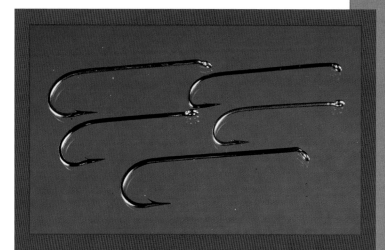

Made of stout wire, hooks for bucktails and streamers come in many varieties. The type of hook used for a baitfish pattern has a big effect on the fly's behavior in the water. Chapter 4 will help you select hooks for bucktails and streamers.

Nymph hooks are also made of relatively stout wire, at least compared to hooks for floating flies. A nymph hook can have an approximately round bend or some version of a Sproat shape. Most manufacturers offer nymph hooks in several lengths. For mayflies, 1X- and 2X-long hooks are more popular; for stoneflies, most tiers use 2X-, 3X-, and even 4X-long nymph hooks. Chapter 6 has some recommendations on which types of hooks to use for various nymphs.

Besides traditional designs, hook manufacturers also offer wet-fly and nymph hooks with curved shanks. A nymph tied on a slightly curved hook such as a Tiemco TMC 200R has a sleek, lifelike look that many fly tiers like. Short, curved hooks make good chassis for scuds, caddis larvae, and pupae, though such flies also work perfectly well when tied on conventional wet-fly hooks. Descriptions of curved hooks, including their sizes, should be regarded as approximations or, in some cases, specimens of poetic license. It's best to buy such hooks in person, so that you can judge how well each model or size fits your needs.

Hooks for bucktails, Muddlers, and streamers are made of wire roughly as heavy as that used for nymph hooks. Streamer irons come in various lengths, descriptions of which can be found in chapters 3, 4, and 5. The style of hook affects how quickly a streamer sinks and how well it holds a fish, and picking hooks for baitfish patterns can require more thought than selecting hooks for dry flies or nymphs.

For bass bugs, fly tiers use a variety of hooks ranging from specialized, wide-gap models to large Aberdeen bait hooks to kinked-shank hooks designed for cork, balsa, or hard-foam popper bodies. The wide-gap "stinger" hooks have their own size scale that bears little resemblance to the scales used for other hooks. Subsurface bass flies are tied on many different types of hooks—streamer models, medium-weight Sproat hooks such as the Mustad 3366, heavy-wire O'Shaughnessy hooks like those used for saltwater flies, and others.

Hooks for saltwater flies vary greatly in shape, shank length, and wire diameter. Some saltwater patterns work best on specific hook models, while others can be tied on a variety of hooks. Workhorse O'Shaughnessy irons such as the Mustad 3407, Tiemco TMC 811S, and Eagle Claw 254 remain popular chassis for many patterns, but the marketplace contains other designs, such as long-shank hooks, circle hooks, and extra-heavy models for big game.

The foregoing are general descriptions of broad categories. Catalogs and web sites can furnish more details. An obsessive hatch-matcher who must have *exactly* the right frame for an imitation of a particular insect has little choice but to capture and study specimens and then compare the bugs to hooks to determine which model has the right dimensions. Thanks to the subtle differences among hooks from different companies, our obsessive friend can probably find just what he wants. On the other hand, a fly tier with a more relaxed approach will find that many hooks, though slightly different, are sufficiently similar to be treated as interchangeable. I tie my bunny-fur nymphs on 1X-long hooks, but I don't care whether the hooks come from Tiemco, Mustad, or Daiichi. And while I'd rather tie a bucktail on a 4X-long iron than on a 6X-long hook of the same overall length, I don't worry about differences between a Mustad 9674 and a Tiemco TMC 9395, both of which are straight-eye, 4X-long hooks. They're not identical, but they are interchangeable, at least in the opinion of fish.

Since I flatten all my barbs, I don't worry about differences in barb height among hooks from various manufacturers. The standard Mustad hooks that have been around for decades have considerably higher barbs than Tiemco or Daiichi hooks have; but after I apply my duckbill pliers to a hook, the difference becomes moot. And since I'm a cheapskate, I don't always spring for premium, chemically sharpened hooks. I like premium hooks for dry flies and nymphs because small hooks are a pain to sharpen. For streamers, bass flies, and saltwater patterns, I generally use the least expensive Mustad hooks and sharpen them with a fine file. On a medium-size or larger hook, I prefer a filed, triangulated point to a conical point. Maybe I'm kidding myself, but a point with three cutting edges seems to penetrate very easily. I triangulate the big hooks on my spinnerbaits and buzzbaits, too, and barely have to strike to drive one of them into a largemouth's yap.

Selecting hooks often entails thinking in relative terms, not absolutes. A hook's overall length matters; if a stonefly's body and head are ¾ inch long, you want a hook with a shank the same length. But there are practical differences between 1X-long and 3X-long hooks that have shanks measuring ¾ inch. The 1X-long model has a bigger gap and longer point, and it weighs more. Do you want the larger gap? Do you need the greater weight? Maybe you do, if you're tying stoneflies for a deep, fast stream that holds very large trout. If you want stonefly nymphs for fishing in a small, shallow mountain stream full of 9-inch trout, maybe you should choose the 3X-long hook.

Similarly, you could tie a 3-inch-long bucktail on a size 4, 6X-long streamer hook or a size 1 saltwater hook. For largemouth bass, pike, and saltwater game, the latter hook is the better choice because of its thicker wire and big gap. For landlocked salmon, the traditional, long-shank streamer iron will probably work better.

You will probably find that you prefer one company's hooks for certain patterns and purposes, another company's products for other jobs, a third hookmaker's goods for still other flies, and so on. You will also find that many flies work equally well tied on any of half a dozen hooks. What matters is that a hook's overall length, gap, weight, strength, shape, and point make it suitable for the job you have in mind.

THREADS

Since it's part of the textile industry, the thread business has standards. Not all companies use them, however. Designations such as 3/0, 6/0, and 8/0 do not always mean the same thing. Size 6/0 Uni-Thread, for instance, is thicker than Danville's Flymaster 6/0 (though it's also considerably stronger). Not all 8/0 threads are identical in diameter, and one company's 10/0 might be the same thickness (and might even be the same stuff) as another outfit's 8/0. Descriptions on labels and in catalogs are, at best, general guidelines.

The only thing to do is try different threads and figure out what you like best. And here I must admit to some laziness. For me, the big difference in fly-tying threads is between nylon and not-nylon. I have a big stock of nylon thread, I'm used to the stuff, and I just plain like its slightly stretchy feel and its bright, translucent appearance. I don't claim that nylon is always better than other materials, because I don't know that it is. But nylon is what my hands are accustomed to working with.

Both of these threads are nominally size 6/0, but four layers of one produce considerably more bulk than four layers of the other. I once received some nominally size 12/0 thread that was in fact bulkier than my usual Danville Flymaster 6/0. Only experience can tell you which threads work best for you.

Because I'm so comfortable with nylon, I haven't experimented with other threads as much as I should have.

Nylon and polyester are the two most popular fibers for fly-tying thread. Nylon has more stretch, and it's usually more slippery than polyester. One must be stronger than the other in a given diameter, but conclusive data is hard to find in the fly-tying business. Bill Merg and Chris Helm compiled tons of data on threads for an article in the Summer 1996 issue of *Fly Tyer,* but even their test results, presented in a table that fills a page and a half of the magazine, don't indicate which material is stronger. For one thing, it's hard to find competitive fly-tying threads that are exactly the same diameter. For another, a thread's construction influences its strength. Some of the nylon threads examined by Merg and Helm seem stronger than roughly equivalent polyester threads; in other cases, polyester seems stronger.

My take on strength is simple: Is the stuff strong *enough* for the job I want to do? On a Hendrickson, Gold-Ribbed Hare's Ear, soft-hackle wet fly, or even a Mickey Finn bucktail, it doesn't matter to me which of the threads I might use—Danville's Flymaster 6/0, size 8/0 Uni-Thread, 70-denier Ultra Thread, Gudebrod's size 8/0 polyester, and a few others—has the highest breaking strength. Any of them will do the job. I'm comfortable with nylon, and so I most often use Flymaster 6/0 or Ultra Thread 70 for trout flies.

A fly tier rarely has to worry about using a thread that has the highest possible breaking strength for a given diameter. Spinning the deer-hair head of a size 4 Muddler Minnow requires a stronger thread than tying in the tails of a small nymph, but any number of threads are strong enough to make the Muddler's head. Which thread you or I like best for tying any fly depends on a number of considerations, of which sheer strength is only one.

Wraps of thread add bulk to a fly, and, as a rule, less bulk is preferable to more. Obviously, a thread's diameter influences how much bulk each wrap adds to a fly, but the thread's construction is just as important. Some threads, such as the Ultra Thread sold by Wapsi Fly, have a "flat" construction. Ultra Thread consists of lots of tiny, continuous, straight filaments. Viewed under magnification, it looks like floss; when wrapped around a hook, Ultra Thread flattens and spreads out, adding relatively little thickness to the shank. Danville's Flymaster 6/0 behaves similarly, though it's not quite so flat and flossy as Ultra Thread.

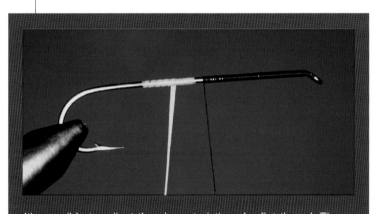

It's possible to adjust the characteristics of a flat thread. These two flat threads are actually identical, differing only in color. The one on the right has been twisted into a hard, narrow strand that's good for bearing down on a clump of bucktail. The thread on the left has been allowed to untwist so that it spreads out and adds practically no bulk to the hook. These threads are Danville's Flat Waxed Nylon. Flymaster 6/0, Ultra Thread 70, Ultra Thread 140, and some other products behave similarly.

Some other threads have a construction that produces a rounder cross section. Both 6/0 and 8/0 Uni-Thread, for instance, have what is called a semibonded construction. The filaments are twisted and, to some degree, bonded together. When wrapped around a hook, size 8/0 Uni-Thread does not flatten out as much as Ultra Thread 70 or Flymaster 6/0. Whether Ultra Thread 70 or Flymaster 6/0 is actually lighter or finer than 8/0 Uni-Thread doesn't matter to me. On a hook, the Ultra Thread produces less bulk. For this reason, flat and nearly flat nylon threads are used by most tiers of fancy-dress salmon flies, on which every tiny bit of extra bulk makes a difference. I don't tie full-dress salmon patterns, but I have learned that I prefer a flat nylon thread for most small trout flies, on which bulk is always a concern.

The flatter or more flosslike a thread's construction, the more control you have over the thread's thickness and behavior. Twisting flat thread by spinning the bobbin makes the thread harder and thinner, and gives it a round cross section that resists flattening under pressure. Those are desirable qualities when you want to bear down hard in one spot, as you might when fastening a clump of bucktail to a hook or spinning a bundle of deer hair. Letting the thread untwist allows it to resume its flat cross section. In that state, the thread adds hardly any extra bulk to the fly, making it excellent for tying off body materials, binding down the butts of tail fibers, and other jobs. Flat thread is more adjustable than other kinds.

As you wrap thread around a hook, you cannot help putting a twist in it. You can demonstrate this by wrapping the entire shank of a nymph hook without stopping. When you finally let the bobbin hang, it will begin to spin as the thread tries to get rid of the twist you put it in. As thread becomes twisted, it also becomes round and hard, which means that it will add more bulk. If you want to add as little bulk as possible with each tying operation, let the thread untwist and flatten. You can speed up the process by noticing the direction in which the bobbin begins to spin and then helping it along.

So, should you always use a flat thread? Not necessarily. Many good tiers prefer Uni-Thread and similar polyester products. Uni-Thread has a rougher texture than that of Flymaster 6/0 or Ultra Thread 70, which makes it grab a hook more quickly, simplifying the jam knot that begins a fly. Polyester threads, particularly those that are twisted or semibonded, are less prone to fraying than flat and nearly flat nylon. Because it grabs small materials well and has relatively little stretch, Uni-Thread can make small flies a little less difficult to tie.

Some tiers, though, like the feel of nylon because it does stretch more than other threads. I much prefer nylon—and fine nylon at that—for tying bucktails and other hair-wing flies. The cumulative pressure of many wraps of thin, slightly stretched nylon locks the material to the hook.

Some tiers prefer certain threads because of their colors. Olive Uni-Thread, for instance, is lighter and greener than olive Flymaster 6/0. Ultra Thread's version of chartreuse is green, whereas chartreuse Uni-Thread is a yellowish color. Danville makes Flymaster 6/0 in a handsome reddish brown that I like for tying certain nymphs. For some dry flies, I prefer Uni-Thread's shade of tan to Flymaster's tan. Using threads from several manufacturers gives a tier a more varied palette.

Personal preferences, then, are as important as anything else when buying thread. Some tiers like stretchy thread; others want as little stretch as possible. One guy wants to keep bulk to an absolute minimum on every fly he ties; another worries about bulk only on small patterns. A tier might prefer one company's version of olive for imitations of the *Baetis* mayflies that hatch from a particular river, but use another company's olive thread for damselfly nymphs. There's nothing wrong with simply *liking* a brand or size of thread.

All that, of course, is of little help to a beginner who owns two spools of thread and wonders what to buy next. For our purposes, and certainly for the purposes of this book, we can put fly-tying threads into three categories: fine, medium, and strong.

Fine threads are those suitable for tying most dry flies, wet flies, nymphs, pupae, scuds, and small to medium-size bucktails and streamers. This group includes Danville's Flymaster 6/0, size 8/0 Uni-Thread, Wapsi's Ultra Thread 70, Gudebrod 8/0, and a number of other products. These threads are not identical—Uni-Thread, for instance, feels and behaves very differently from Ultra Thread—but they all work well for tying most trout flies. A good tier probably prefers one to the others, but he can use any of these threads to tie equally handsome and sturdy Light Cahills, Gold-Ribbed Hare's Ears, Pheasant Tail Nymphs, soft-hackle wets, trout-size Mickey Finns, and hundreds of other patterns.

Medium threads are used when a tier wants more bulk or strength. On a size 2 bucktail, for example, a medium-weight thread builds up a suitably large head more rapidly and easily than a fine thread would. A tier needs a medium thread when he wants to spin a small bundle of deer hair to make a tiny Muddler, a cricket, or one of the Spunduns in chapter 11. Medium threads are also good for Elk Hair Caddis and similar flies tied on size 12 or larger hooks. This group includes Ultra Thread 140 (which is twice as heavy as the 70-denier version), size 3/0 Monocord from Danville, Gudebrod 3/0, and quite a few other products. Thanks to its flat construction, 140-denier Ultra Thread adds relatively little bulk to a fly. When it's twisted, though, Ultra Thread 140 works quite well for spinning small bundles of deer hair or securing the wing of a big Elk Hair Caddis. I'm inclined to put size 6/0 Uni-Thread in this category because it's noticeably thicker than Flymaster 6/0 and strong enough to spin small clumps of deer hair. In the 6/0 size, Uni-Thread is good stuff for tying large bucktails, crickets, most hoppers, small Muddlers, and Spunduns. Uni Products also sells a size 3/0 polyester thread that straddles the line between medium and strong.

Freshwater tiers need strong threads for spinning deer hair. Saltwater fly tiers use these threads for that purpose and for building immense streamers. The strong category includes such products as Danville's Flymaster Plus and Flat Waxed Nylon, Gudebrod G Thread, and A+ Uni-Thread. A few bass-bug tiers use size A rod-winding thread for deer-hair work. For all but the smallest Muddlers, deer-hair bass bugs, and Dahlberg Divers, I'm partial to Flymaster Plus, a heavy (roughly size A) nylon thread.

The strong category also includes threads made with fibers other than nylon and polyester. One of them is Kevlar, which has been on the fly-tying market since the 1980s. Kevlar thread is very strong for its diameter, but it's also coarse and abrasive. It has no stretch at all, a characteristic that gives it a strange, "dead" feel. I stopped tying with the stuff a long time ago, though I occasionally stain a length of Kevlar thread with a permanent marker and use it as a rib on a nymph, a purpose to which Kevlar's abrasion resistance makes it well suited.

Gel-spun polyethylene (GSP) threads are astonishingly strong for their diameter, and for that reason have found favor with many deer-hair tiers. Like Kevlar, gel-spun thread has no discernible stretch. It's slippery, which makes it hard to attach to a hook, and difficult to cut unless it's twisted and held under tension. Because it's so strong, GSP thread can encourage a tier to use too much pressure—enough, sometimes, to slice through a clump of deer hair. For Muddlers, Dahlberg Divers, and most bass bugs, I prefer a stout nylon thread such as Flymaster Plus. But I don't dislike GSP, and many good tiers love gel-spun thread. Try some and make your own decision.

That's my best advice about all threads. If you habitually use nylon, pick up a spool of polyester thread from Uni Products or Gudebrod. If you haven't tied with nylon since Uni-Thread came on the market, try a spool of Ultra Thread or Flymaster. You might find that you have uses for several types of thread.

CEMENTS

At a gathering of fly tiers years ago, I heard someone tell a beginner that using head cement is a waste of time and money. "If it's made properly," this gent explained, "a whip-finish knot won't untie itself. Head cement is a crutch for sloppy fly tiers."

When I had a chance, I took the beginner aside and suggested that he ignore that particular piece of advice. True, a whip finish will not come undone. But gluing the tie-off knot is not why we use head cement. Cement or lacquer seals the head of the fly and protects the exposed thread from abrasion. A fish's mouth can tear up an uncemented head in a hurry.

And cement is *not* a crutch. While it cannot replace good technique, cement can improve the durability of flies. Adding a drop of cement to the butts of a hair wing is not an admission of weakness or an attempt to cheat. It's common sense and a good practice. When you fasten weighting wire to a hook, you should always use cement.

You will need two or three types of cement, depending on whether or not you want your flies to have glossy, elegant heads. The first type is a flexible cement. This stuff has several uses: treating the goose, duck, and turkey quills that provide wing-case material for nymphs; cementing the butts of hair wings such as those of bucktails; reinforcing the bases of some dry-fly wings; and cementing the heads of flies. Dave's Flexament is the most popular flexible cement, though old-fashioned vinyl cement also works well. Both emit powerful fumes and dry quickly, and both require periodic thinning with an appropriate solvent. Flexament isn't nearly so stinky as vinyl cement.

If you want to save a few bucks, you can make a first-rate flexible cement. The next time you visit a hardware store, pick up a tube of Shoe Goo or Household Goop and a small container of toluene. You will also need a small bottle or jar, ideally one with a polyethylene liner in the lid. Hobby shops sell such containers. Squeeze some Shoe Goo or Household Goop into the bottle, filling it about one-fourth of the way. Then add toluene until the bottle is almost full. Use a metal implement to mix the glue and toluene; stir the stuff until all the glue has dissolved. Cap the bottle. The mixture will probably appear cloudy at first, but it will become clearer after it sits for a day or so.

I've been using such homemade cement for about a decade. It's cheap, very strong, and permanently flexible—every bit as good as anything I could buy. Mixing my own gives me control over the cement's viscosity. I use a thin solution for cementing the heads of flies, coating quills from which I will split wing cases for nymphs, and similar jobs. For coating the heads of some bucktails, I use a thicker mixture.

Whether it's store-bought or homemade, flexible cement works perfectly well for sealing the heads of most flies. One coat provides adequate protection to the head of a trout fly; two coats of my homemade cement make a smooth, almost glossy finish.

If you want some of your flies to have a slick, hard, glossy finish on their heads, you will need a good head lacquer. The best head lacquer I've used is a product called Cellire, which comes from England. On a small fly, one coat makes a glossy head; two or three coats make the head look like it is encased in glass. People who tie salmon and steelhead

Flexible cement is the most versatile type. On this nymph, homemade flexible cement (Household Goop thinned with toluene) serves as the coating on the wing case and as head cement.

flies love Cellire for this reason. If you want to try it, check the catalogs of suppliers that carry salmon-fly materials. Other solvent-based head cements and lacquers can produce an equally pretty finish, but they generally require more coats to do the job.

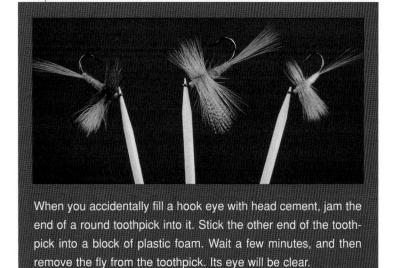

A homemade gadget like this applies head cement more neatly and precisely than a bodkin does. The tool consists of a few inches of No. 4 leader wire glued into a short piece of dowel. It lets you place a tiny drop of cement exactly where you need to.

When you accidentally fill a hook eye with head cement, jam the end of a round toothpick into it. Stick the other end of the toothpick into a block of plastic foam. Wait a few minutes, and then remove the fly from the toothpick. Its eye will be clear.

The importance of a slick, glossy head is a question of taste. Whether the head of a wet fly or nymph has one coat of homemade flexible cement or three coats of Cellire has no bearing on the fly's effectiveness. Some people want all their flies to look as beautiful as possible. Others, like me, are less particular. I'll put several coats of Cellire on the head of a special fly that I want to give to a friend. My nymphs for fishing, however, get one coat of homemade cement.

I'm not a big fan of water-based head cements. Rather than penetrate the thread, they seem to sit on top of it, forming more of a capsule than a finish. Some water-based cements are indeed very watery, forming a thin, fragile coating on a fly's head. They also tend to run back into the materials behind the head. Note that I'm referring to head cements, not to more viscous coatings or finishes. Some water-based coatings, such as Loon's Hard Head and Soft Head finishes, have many uses. But when I want to cement the head of a dry fly or nymph, I use a solvent-based product.

Clear nail polish works pretty well as head cement, and it has the advantage of universal availability. Nail polish's drawbacks are its viscosity (it's usually too thick for small flies) and its tendency to become even thicker once the bottle has been opened. I use it occasionally, but not often. Sally Hansen Hard As Nails seems the most durable nail polish, but not even this product holds up as well as good head cement or lacquer.

As I mentioned in the first chapter, I apply head cement with a homemade gadget consisting of a few inches of No. 3 or No. 4 stainless-steel leader wire epoxied into a handle of some sort, generally a short piece of dowel. This sort of applicator permits very precise placement of a tiny drop of cement, and works much better than a bodkin.

Inevitably, though, we all fill the eyes of some hooks with head cement. That's why it pays to keep a shot glass full of round toothpicks on your tying bench. When you miss your aim or apply too much cement and fill the eye of a hook, jam the end of a toothpick into the eye. Then set the fly aside to let the cement dry. After the cement has dried, remove the toothpick. Make this a habit; otherwise, you will have to waste time trying to poke dried cement out of a hook eye so that you can tie the fly to your leader.

The third type of cement you need is a cyanoacrylate (CA) adhesive, commonly known as superglue. The Super Glue brand works very well for fly-tying applications. Use a CA glue wherever you need great strength or a very tough coating. For instance, use superglue to cement the wraps that hold pieces of weighting wire against the sides of a nymph hook, to coat a wrap of weighting wire on the shank of a streamer hook, or to cement the crisscross wraps that attach dumbbell or bead-chain eyes to a hook shank. Do not use this stuff as head cement. Apply superglue with the tip of a round toothpick.

FINISHES

Many baitfish imitations, particularly those with painted or stick-on eyes, require more than a few coats of head cement. A layer of clear finish protects the eyes of a bucktail or streamer and adds a little bulk to the head of the fly. If it's thick enough and made of the right stuff, a clear coating can also add some weight to the front end of a baitfish pattern.

Saltwater fly tiers have long used two-part epoxies to coat the heads of their flies. Epoxy has a number of advantages. If it's applied properly, it cures to a glass-smooth, hard, tough coating. Epoxy sticks well to a fly's head (it's glue, after all), and it's safe to use over painted or stick-on eyes.

Epoxy does require mixing and some special handling, which might explain why many freshwater tiers don't use the stuff. But epoxy is such a good finish, even on small bucktails, that it's worth learning to use. If you've never tried epoxy or had bad results with it, the following tips will help.

Start with Devcon 5-Minute Epoxy. This product provides more than enough working time to coat the head of a big fly, but it becomes stiff within a few minutes. Squeeze precisely even amounts of the resin and hardener onto a piece of clean, heavy-duty aluminum foil. Use a large paper clip to mix the two parts. Mix the glue thoroughly, stirring the two parts together for at least a full minute.

Use a straightened paper clip, a piece of wire, or a bodkin to apply a thin coat of the mixed epoxy to the head of your fly. Try not to fill the hook eye with glue. If you do smear some epoxy over the eye of the hook, use a round toothpick to remove it.

Epoxy sags until it becomes stiff, which means that you need to rotate a fly coated with it. Serious epoxy-fly tiers have low-speed, motorized curing wheels that turn their flies until the goo hardens, but you can get good results with a spring-loaded wooden clothespin. Clamp the bend of the hook in the clothespin and set it near the edge of your desk, so that the fly's head projects beyond the edge. Within 30 seconds, the epoxy will have sagged and made a lump on the bottom of the fly's head. When you see that, simply turn the clothespin over. Now the epoxy will sag toward the top of the fly's head. I've used this clothespin trick since the 1980s to tie thousands of epoxy-coated flies; chapter 4 has a couple of photos that illustrate it. With Devcon 5-Minute Epoxy, you will have to turn the fly only two or three times before the coating becomes stiff enough to resist gravity.

Once you get the hang of mixing and handling two-part glues, try Devcon's 2-Ton Epoxy. This stuff has a much longer curing time, which means that you can coat four or five flies with a single batch. Obviously, you will have to baby-sit the flies until the epoxy becomes stiff, turning each clothespin as necessary.

If epoxy seems like too much trouble, you can use a one-part coating such as Softex. This product has the consistency of thick syrup (it can be thinned with toluene), and it dries to form a clear, flexible, very tough finish. Although it's easy to use, Softex has two drawbacks. Because of the toluene it contains, it emits nasty fumes that bother some people (and probably aren't good for anyone); also, it will attack and dissolve painted eyes. As a coating for stick-on eyes, however, Softex is great stuff. You can make a similar finish by thinning Shoe Goo or Household Goop with toluene until the glop reaches the desired consistency, about that of cold chocolate syrup.

To cover a head that has painted eyes, use a water-based coating such as Hard Head or Soft Head finish from Loon Outdoors. Both of these are much more viscous than head cement (though not as thick as Softex), and both dry to form a clear, tough finish. Soft Head and Hard Head will not attack painted eyes. They are, of course, suitable for use over stick-on eyes as well.

Some of the acrylic and urethane varnishes sold in craft stores can serve as finishes for the heads of bucktails and streamers. I've had good results with products made by Delta Technical Coatings. Two or three coats are required to build up a slick, glossy finish, but each coat takes only seconds to apply with a toothpick. Although they're very durable, these products need to cure for a few days before going in the water; do not coat the head of a bucktail with acrylic varnish and take the fly fishing two hours later. Their simplicity of application makes acrylic and urethane craft varnishes good choices for small bucktails and streamers.

I can remember tying trout flies on small, offset-point bait hooks. I tied them with size 00 rod-winding thread and cemented their heads with black model-airplane paint. Those were the materials I had when I was a kid, and I made do with them. My ugly flies caught a few fish, too.

These days, we have loads of choices when we shop for hooks, threads, and cements. "Choices" is the key word. Don't let anyone tell you that a certain brand of hook is the only one worth using or that one type of thread is always the best. Experiment with as many products as you can. You will develop preferences—all fly tiers do—but try to remain open to the possibilities offered by the variety of goodies in tackle shops and catalogs.

I have never met Russell Blessing, the Pennsylvania angler who invented the Woolly Bugger. I don't know if Mr. Blessing is surprised, amused, or proud to have devised one of the half a dozen most important flies of the past 50 years. Perhaps he doesn't even think about the Woolly Bugger that way. Maybe he's just happy that so many fellow anglers have caught so many fish with one version or another of his creation.

Listing the fish for which a Woolly Bugger is *not* a good choice is much easier than listing those for which it is. Permit are not good Woolly Bugger customers. Billfish and some other bluewater creatures prefer much larger meals; marabou doesn't come long enough to allow the construction of a foot-long Woolly Bugger. But nearly every other fly-rod gamefish will eat (and has eaten) some incarnation of the Woolly Bugger idea. For trout, bass, panfish, and pickerel, an angler cannot throw a more reliable fly.

Hindsight makes the idea seem obvious: Lash a tuft of marabou to the end of a medium-long hook, and then tie an elongated Woolly Worm on the shank. Considering the age of Woolly Worms—they were called Palmer Flies in Izaak Walton's day, and were old even then—it's remarkable that no one thought of adding the fluffy, wiggly tail until the last third of the 20th century.

What do Woolly Buggers imitate? All sorts of things: leeches, minnows, sculpins, darters, hellgrammites, shrimp, crayfish, and damselfly nymphs, for starters. Sometimes, of course, a Woolly Bugger is simply a good lure, in much the same way that a Mister Twister soft-plastic grub is a good artificial bait. But a thoughtful fly tier can build Buggers that do represent many types of fish food. With its hackle fibers folded back by the pressure of the water and its tail wildly fluttering, a white or pale gray model is a passable imitation of a baitfish. An olive Bugger twitched along the top of a weed bed cons trout looking for damselfly nymphs. Bumped along the bottom of a stream, a brown specimen looks enough like a crayfish or sculpin to fool smallmouths and trout. Tan, olive, gray, and brown Woolly Buggers will catch saltwater fish accustomed to eating shrimp. The standard black model might owe most of its fish-appeal to visibility and motion. Then again, a black Bugger undulating through the water can suggest a leech, and one drifting just above a riverbed can look like a hellgrammite.

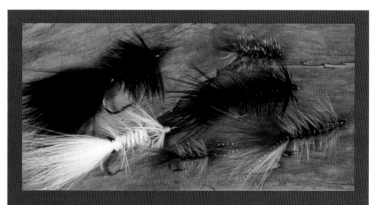

Since they can be tied in a huge range of sizes and colors, Woolly Buggers can appeal to nearly all fly-rod gamefish. A wire rib that secures and reinforces the hackle makes any Bugger much more durable.

These are hard flies to screw up. Even a poorly tied Woolly Bugger will catch fish until it falls apart. A neatly tied fly, however, gives its owner more confidence (it gives this owner more confidence, at any rate). And a well-tied Bugger will last much longer than one that looks like it was assembled by a monkey with neurological problems.

But even a neatly tied Bugger can have a short life expectancy. The weak spot of a typical Woolly Bugger is the stem of the palmered hackle. Although a trout's teeth aren't very big, they can cut the hackle stem, instantly ruining the fly. A pickerel or pike can destroy a beautifully tied Woolly Bugger just by nipping at it. Even the bristles along the edges of a largemouth's yap can abrade an unprotected hackle stem.

The solution is to protect the hackle stem. Rather than build a Woolly Bugger the usual way, with a hackle tied in by the tip and then spiraled forward over the body, we shall tie ours with a hackle wound from front to rear and secured by a counterwound wire rib. In effect, the wire rib stitches the hackle to the body of the fly. Even if a fish cuts the stem at one spot, the feather will not unwind. Half a dozen pickerel can chew on a Bugger made this way without wrecking it (completely, anyway). The front-to-back method of hackling also imparts a skill that we'll use later, on hair-wing caddisflies.

Before we start wrapping hackles and ribs, however, let's look at all of a Woolly Bugger's components.

THE PARTS

A 3X-long hook makes a good chassis for most Buggers. Depending on how you look at it, this is a long nymph hook or a short streamer hook. The Mustad 9672, Tiemco TMC 5263, or anything with similar proportions works fine. For a small Bugger, I'd rather use a 2X-long hook; a size 10, 2X-long iron is about the same overall length as a 3X-long size 12 hook, but the former model weighs more and has a bigger gap and deeper throat.

Except on the very largest Woolly Buggers, there's no need to use thread heavier than 6/0 (or 70 denier, to use Wapsi's system for describing its Ultra Thread). On a real monster, I'll go as heavy as 3/0 Monocord or 140-denier Ultra Thread.

Most tiers wrap the shanks of Woolly Bugger hooks with weighting wire. Trout or smallmouth fishing usually calls for weighted Buggers, but a largemouth angler should carry a few unweighted flies. In shallow water, an unweighted Woolly Bugger is among the best bass flies.

The marabou tail and chenille body do not require much explanation. I prefer the looks of marabou that's not overly fuzzy, but fish seem more open-minded than I. The body material should roughly correspond to the size of the hook: medium chenille for most Buggers, large chenille for the biggest specimens, and fine chenille for the smallest flies.

The best hackles for these flies come from saddle patches—pieces of chicken skins, that is. A package of strung saddle feathers might contain a few hackles suitable for Woolly Buggers, but most will have fibers that are too long. Even a low-grade saddle patch generally has a fair number of good body hackles. A webby hackle with relatively soft fibers is ideal.

Some tiers use black hackles on black Woolly Buggers; others use dark grizzly feathers. If I could have only one or the other (grim thought, that), I'd choose the grizzly. I like the mottled look of a palmered grizzly hackle. Fish also seem to like it. A natural grizzly hackle also works well on olive, brown, tan, gray, and white Buggers; I haven't noticed that color-coordinating their bodies and hackles makes these flies any more effective.

Our Woolly Bugger will have a rib that secures and protects the stem of the body hackle. Fine copper or brass wire works well; these days, fly-tying suppliers sell copper wire with a variety of colored coatings, allowing a tier to use, say, a green rib on an olive Woolly Bugger. In my experience, most fish are happy with a plain copper rib.

Weight the hook according to the depth and speed of the water where you intend to fish. Flies for a big, deep, fast river probably need a lot of weight; those for a slow, thigh-deep smallmouth stream need very little weight, or none. Remember that you can always use a tiny split shot on the tippet to make a fly swim deeper.

TYING TIPS

"Marabou" gets its name from the original source of this fluffy material, the marabou (or maribou or maribout) stork. These days, our pseudo-marabou feathers come from domesticated turkeys. They come in two main varieties: long plumes with fairly thick stems, and short, wide "blood feathers." The blood feathers are more common.

A blood feather can be turned into Woolly Bugger tails in a couple of ways. With most feathers, you can start by stripping some of the uneven, wildly fluffy material from the base of the feather and discarding it. Snip out the tip of the feather, cutting the stem about a third of the way down from the end of the plume. This gets rid of the very short fibers at the tip. Then cut the stem near the butt of the feather, leaving the middle section of the stem with all of its fibers attached. Stroked into a neat bundle, these fibers make a good tail for a typical Woolly Bugger.

You can also cut or strip bundles of fibers from the stem. This approach works perfectly well, but it's a little less convenient than using the middle third (or middle half) of the stem with all the fibers attached. With a large blood feather, you can use both methods: Make one tail by snipping out the middle third of the stem, and make another by cutting the fibers from the remaining butt section of the feather.

Marabou is not a difficult material to use, but the fibers do tend to blow around. On a Woolly Bugger, some of the tail fibers can waft forward and get in the way while you wrap the body, hackle, or rib. Moistening the material will tame it. Dip the tip of your index finger into a cup of water and then stroke the marabou a couple of times. That little bit of moisture will make the fuzzy fibers stick together, making the material less likely to blow around. If you have trouble controlling the stuff, this is a good trick to remember.

Most Woolly Buggers are tied with extra weight on the hook. The weighting wire makes a lump on the shank. When you attach the tail, use the butts of the marabou to smooth out the lump; the photos will give you the idea.

Attach the end of the chenille first, and then attach the end of the rib wire. Leave room for one wrap of chenille *behind* the rib wire; this will simplify winding the rib. Again, the photos show how it's done.

Use nail clippers rather than your good scissors to cut wire. Copper is a relatively soft metal, but it can still harm the edges of fine scissors.

When you wrap the hackle feather, make two turns at the very front of the body. Then wind the feather in a spiral over the body. This gives the hackle a little more density and definition at the front of the fly.

Here's a good trick for securing the rib wire at the head of the fly. After winding the wire over the body and through the hackle, bind it down at the head of the fly with five or six snug wraps of thread. Pull the wire down on the far side of the head, and then pull it toward the rear on the underside of the head. Secure the doubled-back wire with another five or six tight wraps of thread, and then clip the excess. Doubling back the wire this way keeps it from ever pulling out.

These are not complicated flies, and tying them does not involve any tricky techniques. Woolly Buggers are good first flies for beginning tiers. Even if you've been tying for a while, though, I think that you will find the wire rib a good addition to your Buggers.

TYING A TOUGHER BUGGER

We can use the following parts list for a trout- or smallmouth-size black Woolly Bugger.

Hook: 3X long, sizes 4 through 8.
Thread: Black 6/0, 8/0, or 70 denier.
Weight: Fine or medium lead or lead-free wire wrapped around the hook shank.
Tail: Black marabou.
Body material: Medium black chenille.
Rib: Fine or medium copper wire.
Hackle: Black or dark grizzly saddle feather.

Woolly Buggers don't have carved-in-stone proportions. Generally, the tail is about as long as the hook shank, and the hackle fibers are one and a half to two times as long as the hook gap is wide. Feel free, however, to make the tail or hackle a little longer or shorter.

Weighting the Hook

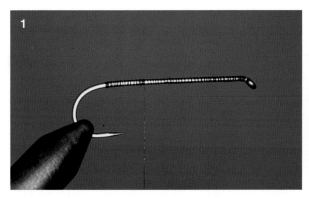

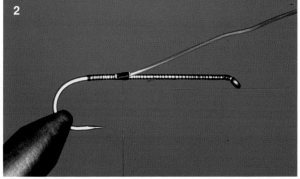

Most Woolly Buggers are tied with some extra weight. If you want to make an unweighted Bugger, skip to step 5. In either case, wrap a foundation of thread on the hook shank. If you're making a weighted fly, advance the thread about a third of the way up the shank.

Use weighting wire (lead is shown here) that's roughly the same diameter as the hook wire. Cut a piece about 3 inches long. Flatten one end of the weighting wire with small pliers. Attach the flattened end to the hook as shown, with the wire pointing forward.

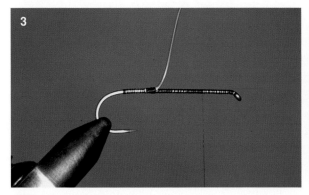

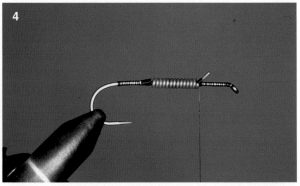

Bend the weighting wire up and out of the way. Advance the thread to a spot about one-fourth of the way back from the hook eye.

Wrap the weighting wire around the shank in contiguous turns. When you reach the spot where the thread is hanging, tie down the end of the wire. Make five or six snug wraps of thread.

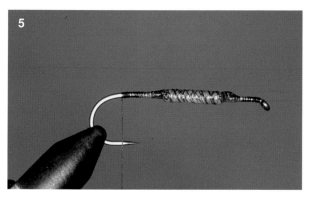

Carefully clip any excess wire. Finish binding down the end of the weighting wire, and then spiral the thread rearward over the weight. Spiral the thread forward and then rearward again, forming a series of crosses on the wraps of weighting wire. Coat the weight and the wraps of thread with head cement, nail polish, or superglue. Note that the weight makes a lump on the hook, but that the ends of the lump are tapered; they are ramps rather than abrupt steps.

Clip the tip out of a marabou blood feather and discard it. Strip the shortest, fluffiest fibers from the butt end of the feather. Stroke all the remaining fibers into a bundle. If you moisten the fibers, as I've done here, they will become a tidy clump that's easy to handle. Hold the marabou above the hook and measure the length of the tail. It should be roughly as long as the hook shank.

Pinch the bundle of marabou against the hook as shown. Your fingertips should be just about even with the tying thread. Make five or six snug wraps of thread, binding the marabou to the hook.

Bind the butts of the marabou along the top of the hook, using them to further smooth out the lump created by the weighting wire. Clip the excess marabou slightly behind the eye of the hook, bind down the stubs, and then wrap the thread rearward to the base of the tail. Note that we've made the lumpy underbody a little smoother (and a little thicker, too, which on this fly is a good thing).

Making the Body

Pinch the last ¼ inch of a piece of chenille between your thumbnail and forefinger. Pull the chenille over your thumbnail to strip off the fuzz and expose the material's thread core. Bind the thread core of the chenille to the hook. (Here, you can see the end of the core sticking up in front of the tying thread. It was completely tied down before the next step.)

Attach the wire for the rib. Leave a little space—enough for one wrap of chenille—between the wire and the base of the tail. This will keep the rib from wanting to slide off the rear of the body; it's a good trick on many flies that have ribs. Advance the thread almost to the eye of the hook, but don't crowd the eye; you will need room for the fly's head.

BULLETPROOF BUGGERS

Wrap the chenille body, making one turn behind the rib wire and then winding the material forward in contiguous turns. Tie down the chenille at the front of the hook, clip the excess, and bind down the stub. Note how the wire for the rib sticks out of the rear of the body. Later, when you wind it, the rib will not want to slide off the rear of the body, and you will have no trouble making the first wrap with the wire.

Strip the fluff from the base of a saddle hackle to expose the stem. Simply pinch a little of the fluff between your thumb and forefinger and pull it straight toward the butt of the feather. The fibers will easily peel off the stem. Then pinch and peel a little more of the fluff, always pulling toward the butt of the hackle. This is how to strip fibers from any feather.

Attach the stripped hackle stem at the front of the body. Bind it down firmly with at least six wraps of thread. Once the feather is securely attached, clip the leftover stem.

Grab the feather near the tip with your hackle pliers. Make two wraps, one right behind the other, at the front of the body. Then spiral the feather rearward over the body of the fly. Wind the feather in the usual direction—that is, wrap it away from you over the top of the hook, and bring it toward you under the hook.

Spiral the feather rearward until you reach the spot where the rib wire protrudes from the body. Let the feather hang; the hackle pliers' weight will keep it taut and in place.

Grab the rib wire, pull it tight, and begin to spiral it forward through the hackle. Rocking the wire back and forth as you wrap it will keep it from mashing down any of the hackle fibers. Keep the wire tight as you wind it forward in a spiral.

When you reach the front of the hook, keep the wire tight with your right hand. With your left hand, pass the bobbin over the hook several times, pulling each wrap of thread tight after you make it. Make at least six wraps of thread. To lock the rib to the hook (always a good idea), pull the wire down on the far side of the hook, double it back under the fly's head, and bind it down again with another six or eight wraps of thread.

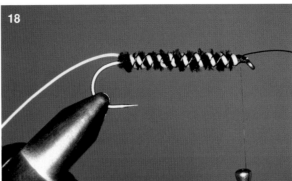

Here's what we've done with the hackle and the wire rib. On this model, the heavy white backing represents the hackle stem, which was spiraled from front to rear. Then the rib (the dark wire) was spiraled forward over the hackle stem. Note how the wire rib crosses the white backing at many points, effectively stitching the backing to the hook. The rib on our fly does the same thing with the hackle stem, making the fly practically indestructible.

Use nail clippers to cut the leftover wire. Finish wrapping the fly's head. Stroke the hackle fibers rearward and hold them out of the way while you build up the Woolly Bugger's head.

Whip-finish and clip the thread. Apply two coats of head cement.

OPTIONS AND VARIATIONS

Obviously, you can make these flies in a huge range of colors and sizes. Black, olive, brown, tan, yellow, white, gray, and chartreuse are all good colors.

The most common variation is the addition of a few pieces of flash material to each side of the tail. Pearlescent Flashabou and Krystal Flash are the most popular materials for adding sparkle to the tails of Woolly Buggers. Go easy with the shiny stuff; two or three strands on each side of the tail are enough.

Woolly Buggers can also be tied with glittery body materials such as Ice Chenille. A reflective, plastic chenille is a good body material for a Bugger that's supposed to represent a baitfish.

Most Woolly Buggers are dark, but patterns tied with light materials—white, gray, or yellow, for instance—are pretty good baitfish imitations. As a Woolly Bugger swims through the water, its hackle fibers lie back along its body, giving the fly a silhouette much like that of a small fish. The fluttering marabou tail adds to the illusion.

A trout-size Woolly Bugger might resemble the smaller fly near the bottom of this photo. Jumbo specimens are excellent flies for bass and saltwater game. The largemouth Bugger on the left is tied on a size 1/0 plastic-worm hook and equipped with a hard-mono weed guard. A size 2, long-shank, stainless-steel hook is the chassis of the saltwater Bugger on the right.

You can also make the rib with fluorocarbon tippet material or gel-spun polyethylene (GSP) fly-tying thread. These materials aren't quite so tough as wire, but they're still tougher than the stem of a hackle feather.

For largemouth bass and saltwater game, you can tie Woolly Buggers on big, standard-length hooks rather than on long-shank irons that have smaller gaps. The wide gap, deep throat, and long point of a standard-length, size 1/0 Sproat or O'Shaughnessy hook are desirable attributes when you fish for largemouths or stripers. Some trout fishermen accustomed to tiny flies shy away from size 1/0 and larger hooks for largemouth bass. But a 12-inch largemouth has no trouble at all inhaling a spinnerbait with a size 4/0 hook or a plastic worm rigged on a similarly large piece of hardware. A Woolly Bugger tied on a size 1/0 or 2/0 Sproat hook is never too big for a bass.

Like nearly all subsurface flies, a Woolly Bugger has more action if it's attached to the tippet with a loop knot rather than a knot that tightens against the hook eye. Try using a nonslip mono loop or a uni-knot instead of a clinch or Trilene knot, and you will see that your flies have more life in the water.

The bucktail is as distinctly American as drag racing or the infield-fly rule. Much of our fly-fishing and fly-tying heritage comes from the Old World, particularly the British Isles, but the idea of adorning a hook with a wad of hair from a deer's tail seems to have been hatched on this side of the Atlantic. It also seems likely that bucktails predate feather-wing streamers. In one of his "Tradition" columns for *Fly Tyer* magazine, John Betts noted that at least a few American fly fishers tied bucktails in the second half of the 19th century. The origin of the feather-wing streamer is generally dated to 1901 and credited to Herbert Welch of Maine, according to J. Edson Leonard's classic work, *Flies*.

Bucktails have great sentimental value to me. The first fly that I tied and actually caught a trout with was a Mickey Finn. I remember that morning in the spring of 1970, and to this day I always have at least one Mickey Finn in my fly boxes, if only as a good-luck charm.

Bucktails of all sorts have great practical value to fly fishers. Big fish eat a lot of smaller fish, and bucktails look like little fish. That's about as deep as we have to go into the theory of bucktail and streamer fishing. In various sizes and colors, bucktails catch everything from white perch to billfish. There probably isn't a more versatile, universally effective family of flies.

The name, of course, refers to the category rather than the material. Some bucktails are indeed made with hair from the tails of deer, but many (perhaps most, these days) are tied with hair from other animals or with synthetic fibers. Calf tail, squirrel tail, goat, kid, llama, craft fur, fox tail, arctic fox, crinkled nylon jig-tying material, polypropylene fibers, coyote hair, yak hair, wool—all are used to make baitfish imitations that fall into the bucktail category. The old Squirrel Tail pattern tied on a size 10 streamer hook is a bucktail; so is a 10-inch-long llama-hair monster built on a size 5/0 circle hook.

On small bucktails, the most useful natural materials are calf tail, squirrel tail, and kid goat. Deer-tail hair can work on small flies if it's fine enough, but deer tail generally works better on midsize and larger bucktails—those from, say, 2 to 4 or 5 inches in length. Five inches is about the maximum length for deer-tail hair (and even that's hard to find), which means that extra-large bucktails have to be made with llama, yak, or any of the long synthetic materials.

We'll concentrate on small to midsize flies from 1½ inches to about 4 inches long, though the tying techniques work for larger bucktails, too. These seem like very simple flies, little more than some tinsel and hair on a hook. That might explain why many tiers get bucktails wrong, or at least not quite right, and why they construct flies that don't swim properly, don't stay in one piece, and don't catch fish. Building a good bucktail involves a number of decisions and skills, some of them subtle and most of them applicable to other types of flies.

THE PARTS

The hook makes a big difference in how well a bucktail sinks, swims, and holds a fish. A 3-inch-long bucktail can be tied on anything from an extra-long-shank, size 6 streamer hook to a standard-length, size 2/0 saltwater iron. Those two chassis will produce very different flies, even if both bucktails are tied with identical materials.

For most trout flies and many smallmouth flies, I prefer a 4X-long hook such as a Mustad 79580 or 9674, Tiemco TMC 9395, Daiichi 2220, or anything with similar proportions. I haven't noticed any practical difference between hooks with straight eyes and those with turned-down eyes, at least for small flies.

I'm not a fan of extra-long hooks, those generally described as 6X to 8X long. Remember that we're talking about the frame of a baitfish pattern, a fly that we want to sink and with which we hope to hook some good fish. Remember, too, that "size" refers to a hook's bend and gap. In this case, though, we're also concerned about the hook's overall length, weight, and proportions.

As I type this, I have three hooks lying to the left of the keyboard. All three are virtually identical in shank length; the difference between the longest and the shortest is no more than a millimeter. One hook is a 6X-long model, one a 4X-long design, and one a 3X-long iron. The 6X-long hook has the smallest gap and shortest point of the three, because it's the smallest size. It is also made of the lightest wire. The 4X-long model is the same overall length, but it has a markedly bigger gap and longer point. It's made of heavier wire, too. The 3X-long hook, made of even thicker wire, has the longest point and biggest gap of the three.

I could tie identical bucktails on all three hooks. The one on the 4X-long hook would sink more quickly than the fly tied on the 6X-long model: The 4X-long hook weighs more because it's made of a slightly longer piece of heavier wire. It will also hold a fish better, thanks to its longer spear and bigger gap; its business end is bigger than that of the 6X-long hook.

The 3X-long hook is heavier still, and it has an even more robust bend and point. For most trout fishing, though, this hook's gap and point are larger than I need. I'd use the 3X-long hook for smallmouth fishing, or for trout fishing in a deep or fast river

Hooks shaped like these are good frames for most freshwater bucktails. The hook at top right is a 3X-long model; the others are 4X-long hooks.

The shanks of these hooks are roughly the same length, and we could tie identical bucktails on all three. The top hook, a 6X-long model, is the lightest of the three. It will produce the slowest-sinking fly. It's also the least likely to hold a fish because of its relatively short spear and small gap. A hook like the middle one, a 4X-long iron, is the best all-around choice for trout bucktails; it's heavier and has a longer point and bigger gap. The 3X-long hook at the bottom is heavier still. Its gap and point might be more than you need for trout fishing, but it's a good choice for a smallmouth fly.

that I suspected held some big fish. For a typical trout-size bucktail, the 4X-long model strikes me as ideal.

These are the types of things a bucktail tier thinks about. The hook isn't merely a place to attach materials. It influences how fast the fly sinks, how deep it swims, and how well it holds a fish. Given a choice between two equally long hooks, I'll generally take the one with the longer point, bigger gap, and heavier wire. Sure, I could add a lot of weighting wire to a relatively light 6X-long hook. But why complicate my tying when I can achieve the same end sim-

Bucktails for trout are typically tied on hooks more or less like the one at top. For bass and saltwater fish, a short, heavy hook like the bottom one is generally a better choice. In smaller sizes (such as this size 4 Mustad 3406), a standard-length O'Shaughnessy hook works very well as the chassis of a trout fly.

ply by using a heavier hook? A 4X-long streamer hook seems a good compromise, at least when I tie trout flies. I will tie a bucktail on a lighter hook with a smaller gap—a 6X-long model, that is—only if a want a fly for light-line fishing in a small stream.

For smallmouth flies, I like 3X-long or shorter hooks—sometimes much shorter. I've had good results with smallmouth flies tied on standard-length O'Shaughnessy and Sproat hooks such as Mustad's 3407 and 3366 in sizes 2 and 4. For largemouth bass bucktails, I prefer heavy, standard-length hooks. The same types of hooks are my choice for most saltwater bucktails, though I like the looks of a Glass Minnow tied on a longer-shank iron such as a Mustad 34011.

I like nylon thread best for tying bucktails because it stretches more than other types of thread. And I tie most bucktails with fine thread, generally the same Danville Flymaster 6/0 or Wapsi Ultra Thread 70 that I use for dry flies, wets, and nymphs. Many wraps of fine nylon thread lock a clump of hair to the hook, making for a durable fly. Using a heavier thread that doesn't stretch results in a less rugged (and less neat) bucktail. On a size 1/0 or larger fly for saltwater fish or bass, I might use heavier thread such as 3/0 Monocord, Ultra Thread 140, or, on a real monster, Danville's Flat Waxed Nylon, a 210-denier thread.

Until the late 1960s or early '70s, fly tiers made the bodies of most bucktails with metal tinsel. That's worth noting because metal tinsel adds some weight to a fly, whereas the plastic tinsels we use nowadays weigh practically nothing. Unless we add extra weight to them, our bucktails are inherently lighter than those tied 40 years ago. If we use relatively light, 6X-long (or longer) hooks and plastic tinsel, we produce flies that weigh considerably less than those tied by, say, Ray Bergman or John Alden Knight. And they'll work less well because they don't sink as quickly or swim as deeply.

So, contemporary tiers often add weighting wire to the hooks of bucktails. That complicates or even prevents making a body with flat tinsel, which is almost impossible to wrap over an uneven foundation. Tiers have solved this problem by finding other body materials such as plastic braids and Mylar tubing, either of which makes a lovely body on a weighted hook. Indeed, many fly tiers now use plastic braids (such as Wapsi's Sparkle Braid, Bill's Bodi-Braid, or Gudebrod's HT Braid) or flashy tubing instead of tinsel on nearly all bucktails, whether or not they're weighted. Compared to tinsel, Mylar tubing or a braid produces a better-looking body with a fish-scale effect. We'll make all three types of bodies in a little while.

A great many animal hairs can be turned into ersatz minnows. Calf tail is a good choice for smaller bucktails, as long as the hair isn't too crinkly. Kid goat also works very nicely on small to midsize flies. Both of these are available in a wide range of colors. Squirrel tail, which comes in a variety of natural and dyed colors, makes handsome flies and works particularly well as the top layer of a bucktail's wing.

The original material, bucktail, comes in many lengths, textures, and colors. Some tails have fine, relatively short hair well suited to smaller flies. Other tails have much longer, coarser hair best reserved for larger patterns. Generally, hair from the bottom half of a tail (the end that was attached to the deer) is coarser and more likely to flare under thread pressure. The best deer-tail hair comes from the top half of a tail (the tip end, that is). Any deer tail, of course, furnishes at least two colors of hair.

For bucktails up to about 2 inches in length, a beginning tier will be happiest with calf tail, squirrel tail, and kid goat. On flies longer than 2 inches, deer-tail hair is hard to beat.

About the only way our forebears could add flash to a fly was to make the body with tinsel, which, being metal, usually tarnished in a hurry. We, however, have a number of products that let us add glitter or flash to the wing of a bucktail. Flashabou and Krystal Flash are the most popular of these materials, but there are many others. Generally, a little of this stuff goes a long way. A size 4 bucktail for trout or smallmouths, for instance, needs only a small clump of Krystal Flash in the wing or a few strands of Flashabou on each side of the hair. A little flash material adds lifelike glitter to a baitfish imitation, but a big wad of shiny plastic can diminish a fly's effectiveness. Used judiciously, any of the modern flash materials can improve the classic bucktail patterns.

Materials such as Krystal Flash and Flashabou add glitter to bucktails. A few pieces of such material can improve nearly any bucktail, whether it's a traditional pattern or a simple, made-up fly like any of these.

TYING TIPS

If you weight the hook, thereby creating an uneven foundation for the body, do not try to use tinsel. Make the body with a plastic braid (Sparkle Braid or Bill's Bodi-Braid, for instance) or woven Mylar tubing. Indeed, you can improve most traditional bucktails by substituting braid or tubing for the tinsel specified in the original patterns.

Should you weight the hook? The answer depends on such factors as the depth at which you want to fish and the speed of the current. If you use a heavy hook, you might not have to add much (or any) weight. Remember, too, that today's sinking and sinking-tip fly lines sometimes obviate heavily weighted flies. Even a fluorocarbon leader can help, since it's denser than a nylon leader. Of course, in a deep, powerful river, you might need to use both a line with a fast-sinking tip and a fly tied with lots of lead wire.

Generally, though, I prefer lightly weighted or unweighted bucktails. They have more life in the water than flies tied with tons of extra weight. If I need to get deeper, I can add weight to the leader or use a sinking line.

Make your bucktails sparse. Most tiers use too much hair. You need only enough material to suggest the shape of a minnow's body. Besides, an overly bushy fly doesn't sink well; in a strong current, a fly with too much hair will swim just under the surface, even if the hook is heavily weighted. When you tie a bucktail with a three-layer wing—a Mickey Finn or Black-Nosed Dace, for instance—be very careful not to use too much hair. Sparser is better.

Don't stack the hair for a bucktail's wing. A wing with perfectly aligned tips will not have a tapered shape in the water. You want a bucktail to resemble a minnow, not a paintbrush tied to a fishhook. But you should clean each bundle of hair to remove short, broken, and curly fibers. After cutting a small bunch of hair from a tail or a patch of skin, pinch the clump about halfway between tips and butts. Stroke the short and broken hairs out of the butt end of the clump. Flick the bundle with a fingertip to loosen any undesirable hairs that you didn't remove by stroking. Then hold the clump tightly at the butt end and look for any hairs that curve away from the others. Pluck out the wildly curly hairs one at a time. The hair is now ready for tying.

Obviously, you want to keep the hair on top of the hook. Accomplishing this is purely a matter of tying technique. After establishing the length of each wing clump, pinch the hair and hook tightly with your left thumb and forefinger (assuming that you're right handed) so that the tips of your fingers are even with the tying thread. As you make the first few wraps, the thread should brush your fingertips. Maintain your tight grip on the hair until you have made 8 or 10 snug wraps of thread. You can slide the tip of your index finger forward a little to keep the hair centered atop the hook as you bind it in place.

Trim the butts of each clump of hair at an angle, forming a neat ramp down to the hook eye. Apply a drop of good cement to the butts before binding them down.

Don't worry about making a tiny head on a bucktail. It's more important to anchor each clump of hair securely. Besides, a larger head adds a little weight to the nose of the fly and provides more room for painted or stick-on eyes (more on these soon).

If you want to tie a full-figured bucktail, such as an imitation of a shad or bunker, build the wing with two or more small clumps of hair rather than one big wad. Constructing the wing with several bundles of hair makes for a tougher, neater fly that's less likely to come apart.

Some bucktail patterns have throats, some don't. A red throat never hurts any baitfish fly, so feel free to add it to any bucktail, even if the standard recipe doesn't call for it. On a Black-Nosed Dace, for instance, I'd rather have a red throat than the red tail specified in the original pattern. Red hackle fibers, a small tuft of wool, and a short piece of floss all make good throats on smaller bucktails. On larger flies, you can make throats with red rabbit fur, a pinch of craft fur, or short pieces of red Krystal Flash.

Conventional wisdom holds that bucktails and other baitfish patterns should have eyes, and I'm inclined to agree. After all, real minnows have eyes, and putting orbs on a bucktail can't possibly make it less appealing to fish. In the old days, fly tiers used lacquer to make painted eyes. Some people still use lacquer, but tiers have found better ways to make eyes. On a smaller bucktail, try the acrylic paints available in craft stores and from some fly-tying suppliers. Seal the fly's head with two coats of head cement, let the cement dry, and then use a finishing nail to apply a dot of white, yellow, or cream acrylic paint to each side of the head. After the irises dry, use a still smaller nail or the head of a pin to make black pupils. Let the pupils dry, and then apply at least one coat of clear finish to protect the eyes. Clear acrylic varnish makes a good top coat. It's available in small bottles in craft stores; make sure that you get varnish that's suitable for exterior use. You can also use any of the water-based fly-tying finishes such as Hard Head or Soft Head from Loon Outdoors.

On larger bucktails, stick-on eyes are faster and easier. They look great, too. Again, seal the fly's head with two coats of cement. Put a stick-on eye on each side of the head. Give the head and eyes at least one coat of Loon's Soft Head or Hard Head, or a coat of Softex, a clear, rubbery substance. Fly shops sell all this stuff.

The toughest and most handsome head coating is epoxy. It's also the hardest to work with, though it's not so troublesome as many tiers believe. The main problem is that epoxy runs and sags until it begins to harden. For this reason, many tiers use motorized curing wheels. A motorized wheel is a dandy tool, but you don't need one. With half a dozen spring-loaded clothespins, you can turn out beautiful epoxy-coated bucktails. After tying three or four bucktails and applying their eyes, clamp each hook in a clothespin. Mix a small batch of Devcon 2-Ton Epoxy, which cures in about 30 minutes. Use a bodkin or a straightened paper clip to apply a *thin* coat of epoxy to the head of each bucktail. Put the clothespins near the edge of your desk, so that the heads of the flies project over the edge. As the epoxy on each fly sags and forms a lump under the head (and it will), simply turn over the clothespin so that the fly is upside down, with its head hanging off the edge of the desk. Now the epoxy will sag toward the top of the head. Keep turning the flies until the epoxy has become sufficiently stiff to resist gravity.

Of course, the entire process goes faster if you use five-minute epoxy (I recommend the Devcon brand). But five-minute goo gives you enough working time to complete only two flies, and then only if you work very fast. With the longer working time of 2-Ton Epoxy, you can coat the heads of four to six flies in one sitting.

BUILDING A BETTER MINNOW

Let's use a version of the well-known Black-Nosed Dace as our sample fly. It's a good bucktail for trout and smallmouths, and its three-part wing furnishes a thorough lesson in bucktail construction. If you can tie this fly, you can tie dozens of others.

We can tie Daces with several types of bodies. Let's start by looking at the three most popular: a traditional tinsel body, a body made with plastic braid, and one made with Mylar tubing. The last two bodies work well on weighted hooks. Then we'll construct the wing, tie in a red throat, and add eyes protected by a clear coat.

Here's the recipe for this version of a Black-Nosed Dace.

Hook: 4X-long streamer hook with either a turned-down or straight eye, size 2 to 6.
Thread: Black Flymaster 6/0, Ultra Thread 70, or a similar nylon thread.
Tail: Red yarn (only with a tinsel or braid body).
Body: Flat silver tinsel with a rib of oval tinsel (the traditional materials); silver plastic braid; or silver Mylar tubing.
Wing: A small clump of white calf tail, kid goat, or bucktail; then a sparse clump of black kid goat or black squirrel tail; then a sparse bundle of brown calf tail or brown bucktail.
Throat: Red hackle fibers, wool, or floss.
Eyes: Painted or stick-on.
Head coating: Acrylic varnish, Loon Hard Head, or epoxy.

A Tinsel Body

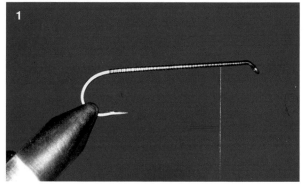

Flat tinsel ribbed with oval tinsel is the traditional body style for this bucktail. Wrap a base of thread from the eye of the hook to the beginning of the bend. Then wrap forward almost to the front of the shank, to about the spot shown.

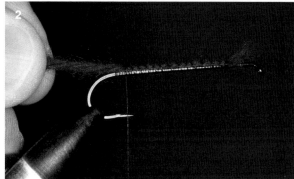

Bind a piece of red yarn along the top of the hook shank. Pulling the yarn taut, as shown, will simplify keeping it atop the hook.

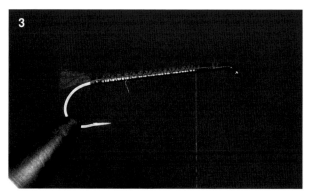

Bind down the rear end of the yarn securely. Spiral the thread forward. Trim the front of the yarn at an angle and bind it down, forming a gentle slope behind the hook eye. You now have a smooth, even underbody.

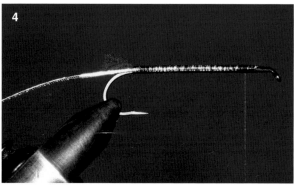

Cut a piece of medium or large oval tinsel (silver, in this case) about 5 inches long. Bind one end of the oval tinsel along the hook shank, but leave a little space between the tinsel and the base of the tail. When you wrap the body, you will make one turn of flat tinsel in this space. Return the thread to the head area of the fly.

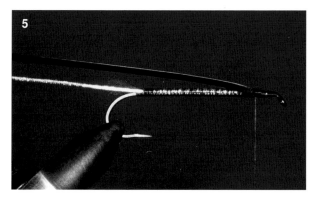

Cut a piece of wide Mylar tinsel about 6 inches long. Mylar tinsel is gold on one side and silver on the other. Attach the tinsel with the gold side facing out, away from the hook. When you start to wrap the tinsel, it will fold and flip over so that the silver side is out.

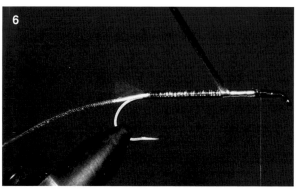

Begin wrapping the tinsel in neat, contiguous turns. As you start the first wrap, the tinsel will automatically fold; the silver side will be out, and the gold side will be in, against the hook.

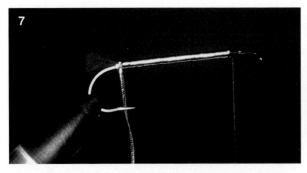

Wrap the tinsel to the rear of the hook. Make one complete wrap between the oval tinsel and the base of the tail—that is, behind the oval tinsel. Wrap the flat tinsel forward, forming a two-layer body, and secure it at the front of the hook. Cut off the excess.

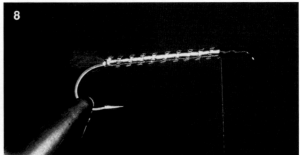

Pull the oval tinsel taut and wind it forward in a spiral. Tie off the oval tinsel at the front of the body and cut the excess. Try to space the wraps so that you can secure the oval tinsel on the underside of the hook rather than on top. Note that the oval tinsel does not come out of the rear of the body. Rather, it emerges from the body slightly forward of the tail, because you made one wrap of flat tinsel between the oval material and the base of the yarn tail. Doing it this way makes the rib much less likely to slide off the rear of the body, simplifying your tying and improving the durability of the fly.

A Plastic-Braid Body

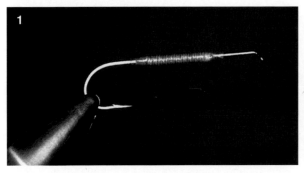

A shiny braid makes a good body on any bucktail, but it's particularly useful on a weighted hook because, unlike tinsel, it does not require a smooth foundation. Weight the midsection of the hook as described in chapter 3, but use white thread to attach, secure, and cover the weighting wire. Give the weighted area a coat of cement.

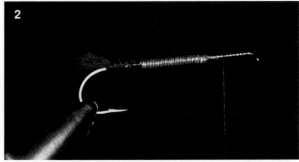

If you want the fly to have a tail, tie in a short piece of red yarn behind the weight. Trim the end of the yarn so that it butts up against the weight, and bind down the end. Bring the thread to the front of the body area, leaving plenty of room for the bucktail's head.

Bind a piece of silver braid (this is Wapsi Sparkle Braid) along the top of the hook shank. Attaching the braid this way helps cover the lump made by the weighting wire and adds some bulk to the body. Bring the thread forward again.

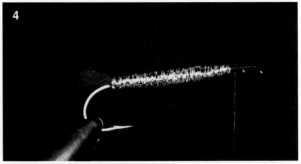

Wrap the braid forward in slightly overlapping turns. Tie off the material at the front of the hook and clip the excess. Bind down the cut end of the braid. This material simplifies making a neat body on a weighted hook, and it produces a plump body with a textured finish.

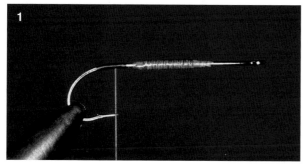

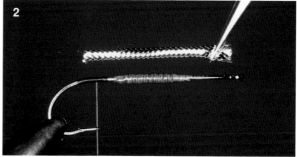

Woven Mylar tubing is another material that's especially handy for making a body on a weighted hook (though it also makes a good body on a plain hook). Weight the hook as described and shown in chapter 3, using white thread to secure and cover the wire. Apply cement to the weighted area. Attach red thread behind the weight and wrap a base of thread slightly past the beginning of the hook bend.

Cut a piece of small or medium Mylar tubing (silver, for this fly) about as long as the hook shank. Remove the core (white cotton string, most often) from the inside of the tubing.

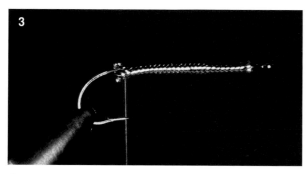

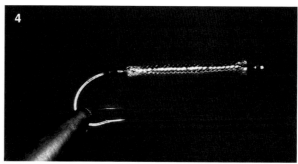

Slide the tubing over the hook. Roll the aft end of the tubing between your fingertips to fray it a little. Push the tubing rearward so that the frayed end straddles the red thread, as shown.

Bind down the rear of the tubing with the red thread. Secure the thread with half hitches or a whip finish; this is one case in which it's good to know how make the whip-finish knot by hand. Give the wraps of red thread a coat of good cement. Since this area of the fly is likely to take a beating from fish teeth, you might want to coat the thread with superglue.

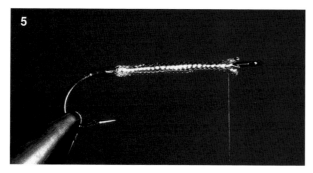

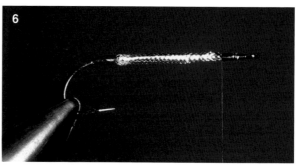

Attach the black thread right behind the hook eye. Slide the tubing rearward on the hook (the material will compress easily) and wrap a short base of the thread on the front of the shank. When you release the tubing, it will return to its original length, and the strands of Mylar will straddle the tying thread as shown.

Bind down the front end of the tubing. This material is very reflective and has a nice fish-scale look. And, of course, it lets you cover a hook made lumpy by the addition of weighting wire.

A Three-Layer Wing

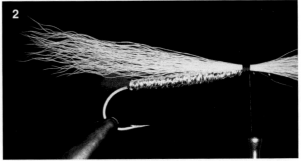

The first key to making this type of fly is using sparse clumps of hair. The second key is holding each bundle of hair tightly in place as you bind it to the hook. Pinch the hook shank and the hair between your thumb and forefinger, with your fingertips even with the tying thread. Maintain your pinch as you begin tying the hair to the hook. As you bind the hair to the hook, slide your forefinger ahead to keep the hair in place on top of the shank. You will use this basic technique on many other types of flies.

Cut a sparse clump of hair (calf tail is shown) and clean out the short and broken fibers from the butt end as described in the text. Hold the hair atop the hook as shown in the previous photo and tie in place with 10 to 12 snug wraps of thread. You have some flexibility in the length of the wing, but, with this type of hook, try not to let it extend more than half a shank length beyond the hook bend.

Trim the butts of the hair at an angle, forming a ramp down to the hook eye. Apply a drop of cement to the trimmed butts. Let the cement soak in for a moment.

Bind down the trimmed butts with neat wraps of thread. Keep the thread tight and wrap another layer back to the rear of the head. Apply cement to the wraps. Cementing each step of the wing will produce a tougher fly—one that will last through many fish.

Cut a small bundle of black hair—just enough to make a dark stripe—and tie it on top of the white. Trim the butts at an angle, apply a drop of cement, and bind them down.

Repeat the process with a clump of brown hair. This is dyed-brown calf tail, but natural brown bucktail works just as well (it's the original material, in fact). Give all the thread wraps a coat of cement.

A red throat is optional, but it's a good addition to nearly any baitfish pattern. You might find it easier to attach the throat if you invert the hook in the vise as shown. This throat is a short piece of red floss; red hackle fibers also make nice throats.

After securing the throat, whip-finish and clip the thread. Give the bucktail's head two coats of cement, allowing ample drying time between the first and second coats.

Eyes and Clear Coat

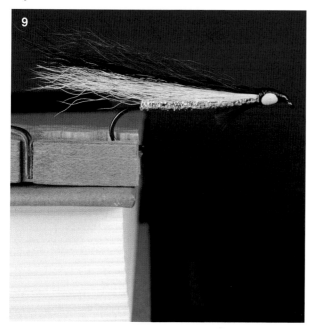

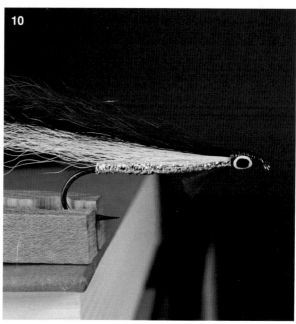

For this operation, remove the fly from the vise. Use a small nail, such as a finishing nail, to apply a dot of yellow, white, or cream acrylic paint to each side of the head. A spring-loaded wooden clothespin can hold the fly while painted eyes dry.

After the irises have dried, use a smaller nail to add the black pupils. Allow them to dry.

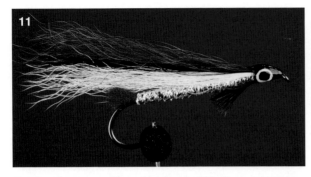

Protect the eyes with a clear finish. This fly received two thin coats of Loon Hard Head finish. Acrylic varnish, available at craft stores, also makes an excellent top coat.

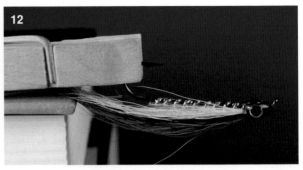

Here's another fly. This one has stick-on plastic eyes protected by a coat of epoxy. Epoxy sags while it cures and can form an uneven or lumpy coating. With a wooden clothespin and a book, though, you can overcome this problem. As the epoxy sags to the bottom of the head, simply turn over the clothespin. Now the goo will sag the other way, toward the top of the head.

Turn the clothespin as necessary until the epoxy becomes stiff. As you can see, prismatic stick-on eyes and epoxy make a handsome head on a bucktail. The epoxy treatment also adds a little weight to the nose and makes the fly very durable.

OPTIONS AND VARIATIONS

The little Dace we've tied is about as complicated as a bucktail needs to be. Two-tone and single-color flies will catch a lot of fish in fresh and salt water. Indeed, a clump of white hair atop a silver body remains one of the most effective lures a fly fisher can cast.

Nearly all fish have a dark-over-light color scheme easily replicated by two bundles of hair. The simple old Squirrel Tail pattern is a good example. Here's a recipe.

Squirrel Tail

Hook: 3X or 4X long, your choice of size.

Thread: Black.

Tail: None.

Body: Silver; any of the three types illustrated above.

Wing: White hair topped with a clump of gray squirrel tail.

Throat (optional): Red hackle fibers or floss.

Eyes: Yellow irises if you paint them; gold if you prefer stick-on eyes.

You can make a gold version of the Squirrel Tail by using (obviously) gold material for the body, yellow hair for the first layer of the wing, and fox squirrel or red squirrel tail for the top of the wing. Yellow and gold flies are sometimes the best choice in off-color water.

Baitfish come in many varieties, nearly all of which can be represented by bucktails. Olive over white or yellow, green over white or yellow, tan over white, brown over yellow, chartreuse over white, and olive or green over gray are all good color schemes. Match the thread to the color of the top of the wing; that is, use olive thread to tie an olive-over-white bucktail and brown thread for a brown-over-yellow one. Give all of them red throats and painted or stick-on eyes.

Silver and gold are the most popular colors for bodies, but tinsel, braid, and tubing also come in pale, translucent varieties called pearlescent or simply "pearl." Pearlescent materials make superb bodies. Most of them, however, allow the color beneath them to show through. When you use pearlescent tinsel or braid, construct the body of the fly with white thread. After finishing the body, switch to darker thread for the wing.

A little Flashabou or Krystal Flash will brighten up any bucktail that's supposed to represent a shiny minnow. Flashabou is essentially very fine, flexible plastic tinsel. I like to tie two or three pieces of it on each side of a bucktail's wing. Krystal Flash is a stiffer, crinkled material. I generally treat it like hair, sandwiching a small bundle between the layers of a bucktail's wing.

Don't overlook attractor patterns. In stained or dirty water, a pink, hot orange, or chartreuse bucktail is often more visible than one that looks like a real minnow. A

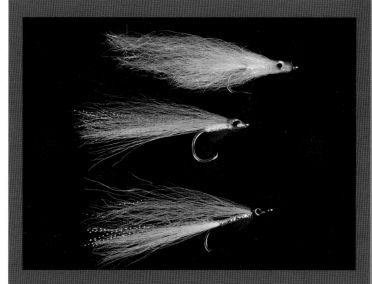

Once you acquire the basic skills of tying bucktails, you can easily make big baitfish for bass or saltwater game. The top fly is made with llama hair; the other two are true bucktails. All three are on size 1/0 hooks, and they'll catch largemouths, stripers, bluefish, seatrout, pike, big pickerel, redfish, and scads of other fish.

big, black bucktail sometimes takes fish when nothing else draws a strike. Black is a particularly good color in dirty water and at night. Largemouth bass, smallmouths, and stripers are all fond of black flies.

And don't overlook simple, commonsensical solutions to fly-tying and -fishing problems. During the 1990s, I had the pleasure and privilege of exchanging letters and a few flies with H. G. "Tap" Tapply, the great outdoor writer whose work adorned the pages of *Field & Stream* for several decades. A few years before he passed away, Tap sent me a little box that contained a pair of bucktails of the type he used for bass fishing. The flies consisted of hair tied to long-shank hooks—no tinsel on the shanks, no tails, no throats. Just bucktail bound to hooks.

The box also held a tiny, neatly typed note that said, "No bodies on bucktails. On account of pickerel, you know." It was classic Tap: not one unnecessary word, and a practical solution

The Squirrel Tail (top) and Mickey Finn are two classic bucktails that continue to catch fish. Both, incidentally, will work in salt water, too.

"No bodies on bucktails" was Tap Tapply's advice on tying flies that might be taken by either bass or pickerel. It's sound advice. If your flies might end up in the yaps of toothy critters, omit the fancy bodies.

to a problem. A pickerel, pike, or bluefish can instantly shred the neatly tied body of a bucktail. So, don't put bodies on flies likely to end up in the yaps of toothy fish. Attach some hair to the front of the hook, add a little Krystal Flash or Flashabou to the wing, and, if you feel ambitious, give the fly eyes.

There is no end to the possibilities of bucktails. Pattern books can supply scores of recipes; an average imagination can create hundreds more. Whether you fish for crappies or tarpon, you can use bucktails. If any category of flies lends itself to creativity, this one does.

But while you're having fun creating, tie a few specimens of the following pattern.

Mickey Finn

Hook: 4X long, any size.
Thread: Black.
Body: Flat silver tinsel.
Rib: Oval silver tinsel.
Wing: A small clump of yellow hair, then an equally small clump of red hair, and then a bundle of yellow hair equal to the thickness of the first two clumps.

That's a Mickey Finn. For a while in the 1930s, it was the most popular fly in this hemisphere. It still has powerful magic and, for some of us, great sentimental value.

The first flies I tied that consistently caught fish were, roughly speaking, Muddler Minnows. I do not claim that they were good Muddlers. They were lousy flies, crude and misshapen, made with strange materials and quick to fall apart, obviously the work of a kid with more imagination than talent. But they caught fish, sometimes even better than bait did. Fly fishing suddenly began to make sense. Practical lad that I was, I even tied a bunch of quasi-Muddlers on jig hooks and gave them split-shot heads. I could cast them with my Abu Garcia ultralight spinning rod, and great was the suffering I inflicted on yellow perch.

Don Gapen's original Muddler Minnow has probably spawned more offspring than any other fly has. Millions of fly fishers have caught countless trout and bass with Muddler Minnows, Marabou Muddlers, Spuddlers, and all sorts of Muddlerish variations. Salmon and steelhead anglers have their own versions of this marvelous fly. Eric Leiser's Angus flies, named in honor of Angus Cameron, Leiser's editor at Knopf and a great angler in his own right, have caught fish from Alaska to Key West. Lou Tabory's Snake Fly has long been a standard among striped bass and bluefish anglers. Sandy Moret's Tarpon Muddler is just one of the many hair-headed flies that backcountry anglers use for tarpon.

Scores, perhaps hundreds, of Muddler-style flies exist. They all share a distinctive feature, a head made of spun and trimmed deer (or sometimes elk) hair. And they are all uncommonly effective flies. Maybe a big deer-hair head makes a fly more visible or gives it a more convincing silhouette. Or maybe, as many have claimed, a Muddler head "pushes water" and creates pressure waves that fish can feel in their lateral lines. Whatever the reason, Muddlers are reliable flies for nearly all gamefish.

And that's why nearly every fly tier wants to make them. Most tiers, though, have trouble with Muddlers. Some struggle with them for years, never getting the hang of the deer-hair head. Oddly enough, I took to tying Muddlers as naturally as a congressman takes to influence peddling. It probably helped that I didn't know that Muddlers are hard flies. And it also probably helped that, 30-odd years ago, I had only two types of thread in my tiny fly-tying kit: some very fine Gudebrod nylon I'd filched from my mother's kit, and a few half-empty spools of rod-winding thread. I figured that the fine stuff was only for tiny flies, which I didn't believe would catch fish anyway, and used the rod-winding cordage for tying most flies. Three-ply, size A thread does not make a particularly handsome wet fly or streamer (especially when one uses model-airplane glue as head cement, which I did), but it proved more than strong enough for spinning little bundles of deer hair. When I started making Muddlers, I'd never seen an actual specimen of a proper, well-tied one, and so the nightmare mutants that came from my vise looked pretty good to me.

I had unwittingly stumbled on one of the secrets of tying Muddlers: Use strong thread for the deer-hair work. I also made the tying easier by simplifying the dressing. That wasn't deliberate, of course. My selection of materials was small, and my knowledge of patterns came from looking at tiny pictures in catalogs. Through ignorance, I achieved bliss. And I caught a lot of fish.

I stopped tying flies for a while (college, beer, girls—the usual distractions), and when, years later, I started again and tried to learn to how to make "good" Muddlers with proper materials, I ran into all the

This is the secret of making the Muddler less miserable to tie: Treat it as two distinct projects. Tie the tail, body, and wing with fine thread, leaving ample room for the deer-hair head. Then switch to heavy thread for the deer-hair work.

usual problems. Sometimes there wasn't enough room for the head, sometimes the head came out loose and fragile, sometimes the thread broke. I worked at it and eventually learned how to make a pretty good standard Muddler. Then I kept working at (or monkeying around with) Muddler-style flies, largely abandoned the standard version, and, in time, settled on the method and flies that are the subject of this chapter.

My advice to beginning or struggling Muddler tiers boils down to this. First, let the classic version wait until later. Learn Marabou Muddlers first—and I mean master them—and then tackle the big turkey-strip wings of the traditional pattern. Second, treat the fly as two discrete projects: a simple marabou streamer tied with red 6/0 thread on the rear three-quarters of the hook, and then a deer-hair head tied with heavy thread on the front one-fourth of the shank. Done that way, a Marabou Muddler presents little difficulty.

Why red thread for the body and wing? Because the thread wraps securing the marabou are often visible through the deer-hair collar of the finished fly. If those wraps are bright red, they suggest the gills of a baitfish. Parts that are visible might as well serve a purpose.

And speaking of parts, let's look at them.

THE PARTS

Use a heavy-wire, 3X- or 4X-long hook. A 4X-long model is good for most Muddlers; it has plenty of room for both the body and the deer-hair head. For a small Muddler, try a 3X-long hook; it's slightly heavier than a 4X-long model of the same overall length, and it has a bigger gap.

Use red Flymaster 6/0, 70-denier Ultra Thread, or something equally fine for tying the body and wing. The body can be any of the types described in the previous chapter: tinsel, plastic braid, or Mylar tubing. Since most Muddlers are tied with extra weight, you will find a braid or tubing easier to use. Chapter 4 shows you how to make the body.

The wing is a tuft of marabou, like the tail of a Woolly Bugger. Traditionally, Marabou Muddlers have been tied with peacock-herl toppings. I don't make them that way. Herl is fragile stuff, and I don't like how it looks with marabou. If I want a two-tone, dark-over-light wing, I make it with two colors of marabou.

My favorite thread for deer-hair work is Danville's Flymaster Plus, a 210-denier nylon that's very strong and easy to work with. Flat Waxed Nylon also works well, as long as you spin the bobbin to tighten the thread so that it doesn't spread out like floss. Although hardly any fly tiers use it anymore, size A rod-winding thread is still good stuff for spinning deer hair. On a very small Muddler that doesn't use much hair, size 3/0 Monocord, 140-denier Ultra Thread, or size 6/0 Uni-Thread (which is both thicker and stronger than 6/0 Flymaster) is usually strong enough.

I use nylon threads for almost everything because I simply prefer the feel of them. Nylon stretches a little, and I like that. Other tiers have different views. Many prefer to use a polyester thread for deer-hair work, and quite a few favor the new gel-spun polyethylene (GSP) threads, which are astonishingly strong. A few, I suppose, still use Kevlar, though I've always hated that stuff. As you learn to work with deer hair, try a variety of strong threads. Remember, though, that an extremely strong thread, such as a GSP product, might encourage you to pull so hard that the thread cuts through the deer hair. That's not the thread's fault, of course; but tying with excessive pressure is more likely to happen with a GSP thread than with heavy nylon. Try the Flymaster Plus for your Muddlers; you won't be disappointed.

The head of a Muddler calls for short to medium-length, moderately coarse deer hair. Hair about 1½ inches long is good for most Muddlers. Very large flies, of course, can use longer, coarser hair, and the smallest Muddlers are best tied with shorter, finer hair. Selecting deer hair is a skill that comes with experience. When in doubt, ask someone at a fly shop or catalog house for help. Tell the salesperson exactly what you intend to use the hair for, because the term "deer hair" covers a lot of territory. The most important thing is to use deer hair that will compress and stand up (or "flare") under thread pressure.

TYING TIPS

Everything aft of a Marabou Muddler's head is pretty easy. When you tie a trout-size Muddler—size 8 up to size 4, say—the main thing is to make sure that you leave at least the first one-fourth of the hook shank bare as you make the fly's body and attach the wing. Do not let so much as a single wrap of the red thread encroach on the first quarter of the shank.

Construct the body as you would on a bucktail (see the previous chapter), but restrict it to the rear three-fourths of the hook shank. You will probably find a braided material easiest to use. After tying in the marabou wing, whip-finish and cut the red thread. Give the exposed thread wraps a couple of coats of good head cement.

Many tiers have trouble with deer hair because they never practice with it. Having only a vague theoretical idea of how the material behaves, they try to spin Muddler heads as their first exercise in using deer hair. This is a bit like wanting to learn to double-haul with a 12-weight outfit as one's first casting lesson. No wonder they have problems.

The way to learn to spin deer hair is to do just and only that: spin it, without trying to make a fly. Deer hair is inexpensive, and using two dollars' worth of it to learn the technique is a good investment, not a waste of material. So, let's practice.

WORKING WITH DEER HAIR

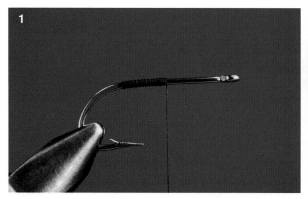

Clamp a big, sturdy hook in your vise and pop a spool of Flymaster Plus or a similarly strong thread in your bobbin. Tie on at the midpoint of the hook shank. Wrap a base of thread to the rear, and then wrap forward to the starting point.

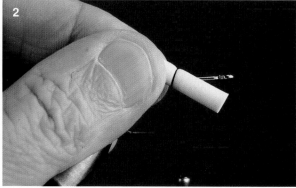

I'm using this foam cylinder to show how to hold a clump of deer hair that you want to spin around the hook. Hold the material at an angle on the near side of the shank. Make two wraps of thread around the material and the hook shank. Use very little pressure as you make these wraps; note that the thread is barely denting the soft foam.

Now let's try it with the real thing. Cut a clump of deer hair about the thickness of a wooden pencil. Stroke the short hairs, broken fibers, and fuzz out of the butt end of the clump. Then put the clump, tips down, in your hair stacker.

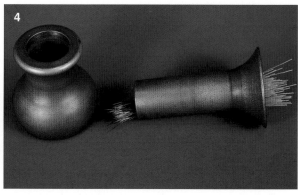

Tap the bottom of the hair stacker on your desk several times. Tip the stacker on its side and separate the halves. The tips of the hairs will be neatly aligned.

Grab the hairs by the tips and carefully remove the bundle from the stacker's tube. Hold the clump of hair in the middle and trim the butts straight across. You now have a tidy bundle of hair that's even on both ends.

Hold the hair at an angle on the near side of the hook. Make two soft wraps of thread around the hair and the shank. Note that these wraps do not compress the hair.

Begin tightening the two wraps of thread. Tighten the wraps smoothly rather than with a sudden jerk. As the thread encircling the hair begins to bear down, the hair will start to flare.

Open your fingertips a little at a time as you continue to tighten the thread. Release the hair completely before the thread wraps are tightened all the way. The hair will continue to flare, and it will spin around the hook as you let go of it.

Keep the thread tight and make another three or four wraps in exactly the same spot. These wraps both secure the hair and continue to distribute it around the hook shank. If all goes well, the hair will now surround the hook.

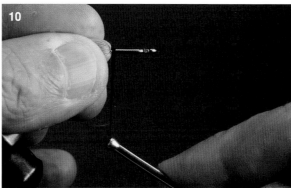

Maintain some tension on the thread while you stroke the butts of the hair rearward. Gather all the hair with your thumb, forefinger, and middle finger and pull it to the rear. Angle the thread slightly forward and make a few tight wraps around the hook shank right in front of the hair.

Prepare a second bundle of hair; this one can be a little smaller than the first clump. Hold it as shown, at an angle on the near side of the hook. As you did with the first clump, make two soft wraps around the hair and then begin tightening the thread.

Keep tightening the thread as you let go of the hair. Make another three or four tight wraps in exactly the same spot.

Gather the butts of the hair and pull them rearward. Angle the thread slightly forward and make several snug wraps around the hook shank in front of the hair. Hold the hair out of the way and secure the thread with a whip finish.

Clip the thread. You can practice shaping a deer-hair head by trimming most of the hair into a bullet shape, leaving a collar of hair at the rear.

After you finish the first spinning exercise, pick up a razor blade and slice all the material off the hook. Then repeat the entire process. Slice all the hair and thread off the hook again, and repeat the exercise once more. Do it all again. And again.

You will have trouble spinning hair the first time you try. So has every other fly tier on the planet. It's not an easy thing to do. Persevere and have patience with yourself, and you *will* master this valuable skill. I can only describe working with deer hair as a "Eureka!" experience—you will struggle and curse and fail, and then, suddenly, you'll get a bundle of hair to roll around the hook. You'll have less trouble with the next clump, and even less with the one after that. By the time you've used all the material on a 4-square-inch patch of skin, you will be able to spin two clumps of deer hair with little or no trouble.

The main thing is to *practice* on a big, bare hook until the procedure begins to work for you. Learning this way is considerably less frustrating than bollixing up one fly after another. Some people become fairly proficient in one evening; most tiers need several practice sessions before they can make deer hair do what they want. Remember that you're not in a race with anyone.

TYING A TWO-STAGE MUDDLER

Once you can spin and trim a two-clump head reasonably well, you can build a complete Marabou Muddler. In time, your skills with deer hair will increase and you will learn how to make denser heads and two-tone heads. Right now, though, let's concentrate on tying a simple marabou streamer and putting a deer-hair head in front of it. If catching fish is your main concern, you don't have to learn how to make Muddlers any fancier than this one.

Here's a general recipe for a Marabou Muddler.

Hook: 4X-long streamer model, size 4, 6, or 8.

Threads: Red Flymaster 6/0 for the body and wing; black, brown, or gray Flymaster Plus for the deer-hair head and collar.

Weight: Lead wire on the hook shank (see chapter 3). Be sure not to wrap any weighting wire on the front one-third of the shank; you will need this space for other purposes.

Body: Plastic braid or Mylar tubing (see chapter 4).

Wing: White, gray, tan, brown, or mottled marabou.

Collar and head: Natural deer hair, spun and trimmed.

Tail, Body, and Wing

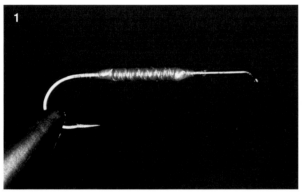

Weight the hook as you would for a Woolly Bugger (see chapter 3), but be sure to leave plenty of room at the front of the shank. Just to be safe, leave the front one-third of shank bare. Give the weighted area a coat of cement; superglue (CA adhesive) is best for this operation.

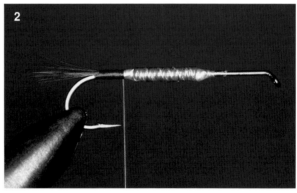

Attach red thread behind the weight. Make the tail with a hefty clump (or two smaller clumps) of red hackle barbs. Trim the tail butts carefully, so that they help smooth out the lump at the rear of the weighted area.

Attach a piece of shiny plastic braid and wrap it to make the body, just as you would on a bucktail (see chapter 4). Work carefully—you must leave the front one-quarter to one-third of the hook absolutely bare.

Tie on the marabou wing. This example has a two-tone wing of brown and tan marabou. Bind down the trimmed butts of the marabou, whip-finish the thread, and clip it. Give the exposed wraps of red thread two coats of good head cement or lacquer, and let them dry before proceeding.

Spinning the Head

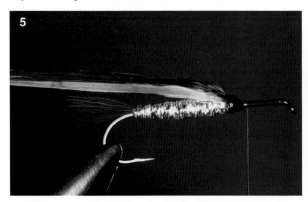

Moisten the wing so that the marabou fibers cannot waft around and get in your way. Attach the Flymaster Plus thread (or whatever you use for deer hair) behind the hook eye and wrap a neat, smooth layer of thread back to the red "gills."

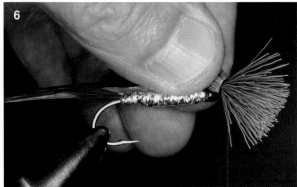

Prepare the first bundle of hair according to the instructions above. Hold it at an angle on the near side of the hook. The tips of the hair can be long enough to reach the point of the hook, but they shouldn't be any longer than that. Make two soft turns of thread around the hair and the hook shank. Begin tightening the thread.

Release the hair as you continue to tighten the thread. Pull the thread all the way tight and make another few wraps in exactly the same spot. It's okay—good, in fact—to support the hook with your left hand while you tighten the thread. There's an old myth that deer hair will spin only on a naked hook shank. Baloney—it will spin perfectly well on a smooth, one-layer base of thread. This clump did.

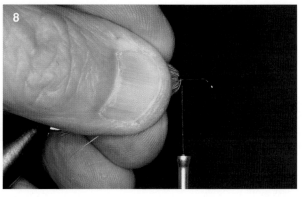

Gather all the butts and pull them to the rear. Angle the thread slightly forward and make three wraps against the base of the hair.

Cut a clump of hair a little smaller than the first bundle. Stack the hair, trim the butts, and spin it as you did the first bunch.

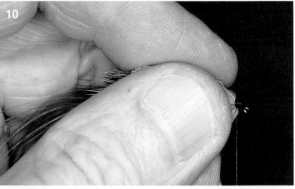

Pull all the hair back and make several tight wraps of thread behind the hook eye. Hold the hair out of the way and secure the thread with a whip finish or several half hitches.

Clip the thread. All the hard work is done. And by the time you've tied half a dozen of these flies, the work is no longer particularly hard.

Begin by roughing out the shape of the head. Use very sharp, fairly sturdy scissors. Trim the bottom first, then the top, and then the sides. You will probably find it easier to remove the fly from the vise to trim the hair; I put it back in the vise so that I could shoot the photo. Don't trim all the hair—leave some of the tips of the first bunch so that the fly has a collar. The collar on this fly is as long as a Muddler's collar should be; many tiers make them shorter.

Use the tips of your scissors to trim the hair into a conical shape. Trim from front to back, taking care not to chop off the hairs that form the collar. Keep the head symmetrical when viewed from above. Some anglers prefer Muddlers with bulbous heads like this one.

Other tiers, and I'm one, prefer to give the head more of a wedge shape. If you're careful, you can use a double-edged razor blade for most of this work. That's what I did here; note how flat the bottom of the head is. A head shaped like this helps the fly to dive. When you're done trimming, cement the whip finish and apply a little cement to the underside of the deer-hair head.

OPTIONS AND VARIATIONS

Muddlers come in so many varieties that a creative and ambitious fly tier could probably make nothing else for a year and still not exhaust all the possibilities. Besides marabou and the original materials (squirrel tail and turkey-quill slips), Muddler wings are made with many furs, hairs, and feathers. Even with simple Marabou Muddlers, there's plenty of room for innovation and creativity.

These days, "marabou" feathers come from domesticated turkeys and are dyed in a huge range of colors. Wild turkeys have some mottled tan and brown marabou plumes

The two-stage, two-threads approach works on Muddlers of all sizes. The top fly has a few pieces of holographic Flashabou on each side of its wing; flash material is a worthwhile addition to any baitfish fly.

Most trout-size Muddlers are tied on 3X- or 4X-long streamer hooks, but big patterns for bass, pike, and saltwater fish are generally tied on standard-length O'Shaughnessy or Sproat hooks. Although it's built on a size 1 saltwater iron, this pattern is constructed like its smaller cousins.

that make superb sculpin and darter patterns. The rump of a ring-necked pheasant has some soft, marabou-like feathers that also work beautifully on Muddlers tied to represent dark, drab baitfish. Even chickens have soft, fluffy feathers that can be turned into wings on small Muddlers. Barred chicken marabou (Chickabou is the trade name used by Whiting Farms) makes a handsome, mottled wing on a size 6 or smaller fly. On a dark fly that mimics a sculpin, a gold body generally works best.

The same materials that add glitter and flash to bucktails work on Muddlers, too. Adding a few strands of Flashabou or Krystal Flash on each side of the wing often improves a Marabou Muddler. Silver flash is good on a white Muddler, and gold flash looks good on a brown, tan, yellow, or olive fly. Pearlescent flash material will work on nearly any pattern. Purple or blue flash makes a nice addition to a black Muddler, particularly one tied for bass fishing.

Although most Muddlers are tied on long-shank hooks, flies for saltwater fish, pike, or bass can work better if they're built on big, standard-length Sproat or O'Shaughnessy hooks. For bass fishing, I'd rather use a Marabou Muddler tied on a size 1 Mustad 3407 (or any similar O'Shaughnessy design) than an equally long fly made on a size 4 streamer hook.

Marabou, of course, doesn't come long enough to permit the construction of very large flies. On a size 1/0 saltwater hook, a tier with good marabou can make a fly a bit more than 3 inches long. But that's big enough to imitate many types of bass, pike, striper, snook, redfish, and tarpon forage. If you need a Muddler that's as long as a dollar bill, you can make the wing with llama hair, yak hair, any number of synthetic fibers, or long hackle feathers. Attach the hair, fur, feathers, or whatever at the bend of the hook, add some flash material, and spin the deer-hair head and collar on the front half of the hook shank. Billfish anglers have found ways to make tandem-hook Muddlers that are a foot long.

Very small Muddlers are deadly trout flies, particularly in small streams. I've had great luck with tiny Marabou and Bunny Muddlers tied on size 8 nymph hooks. The challenge with a small Muddler is making it heavy enough to sink well; there's just not room for much weighting wire on the hook shank. A partial solution is to make the body with medium-size copper wire instead of a plastic braid or tinsel. Even so, a baby Muddler often needs the help of a small split shot on the tippet.

Some tiers don't bother weighting Muddlers at all, arguing that it makes more sense to crimp a split shot on the leader right against the nose of the fly. The argument makes a lot of sense. Putting the weight at the nose of the fly rather than in the body counteracts the natural buoyancy of the deer-hair head and improves the fly's balance, making it dive during a pause in the retrieve.

A copper or brass bead has the same nose-weighting effect and looks a lot better. Slide a large bead onto the hook and shove it all the way up to the hook eye, and then tie the tail, body, and wing as you would on any Muddler. Spin the deer hair between the base of the wing and the metal bead. Whip-finish the thread behind the bead, and then trim the head to shape. This method of tying is a mite awkward the first time you try it, but the result, a Bead-Nosed Muddler, has a marvelous action in the water.

An unweighted Marabou Muddler tied on a light hook functions like a slider. Use a relatively light Aberdeen hook such as a Daiichi 2460 or 2461 or a Mustad 3261 or R52S, and make the fly's head a little more bulbous than usual when you trim it. Treat the head with floatant and, depending on the size of the fly, you will have a first-rate slider for largemouths, smallmouths, big panfish, or pickerel.

Conventional wisdom says that baitfish patterns benefit from having eyes. While I'm not convinced that Muddlers are really improved by the addition of eyes, I put eye

Tiny Muddlers (these are tied on size 8 nymph hooks) don't weigh much. To help them sink, make their bodies with copper wire rather than tinsel or plastic braid.

Fly-tying beads make fine nose weights for Muddlers. Slide a bead onto the hook, and then tie the tail, body, and wing as you normally would, leaving enough room for the fly's head.

Switch to heavy thread and spin the deer-hair head. Whip-finish the thread just behind the bead. Trim the head so that it tapers down to the diameter of the bead. Muddlers tied this way dive very well.

A black permanent marker lets you easily add eye spots to Muddlers. Whether such details impress the fish is hard to determine—but they can't hurt.

spots on some of mine on the theory that they can't hurt. On a Muddler, the simplest way to add eyes is to use a black Sharpie marker to make a dot on each side of the deer-hair head. Jab the tip of the marker into each side of the head and let the waterproof ink soak into the hair. This isn't the most sophisticated way to make eyes on a fly, but it's easy and fish seem to like it. On big Muddlers for bass or saltwater fish, you can use epoxy to attach three-dimensional plastic eyes.

If there's a limit to what can be done with Muddlers, fly tiers have yet to find it. And even less-than-perfect Muddlers, like those sorry specimens I tied as a kid, will catch fish as consistently as anything else you can throw. Don't be afraid of the deer-hair work. If you treat a Muddler as two distinct tying projects, you will have no trouble mastering this uncommonly useful construction.

How many nymph patterns does a fly fisher need? A lot, because the larvae of aquatic insects come in many sizes, shapes, and colors. On the other hand, one style of nymph—one *construction*, that is—can cover most mayfly larvae, many stoneflies, and, in a pinch, even damselflies. The nymph patterns in my fly boxes vary a great deal in size, color, proportions, and materials, yet nearly all of them are built the same way.

That's hardly a novel idea, of course. But it brings up a distinction that merits clarification. A fly *pattern* consists of all the details—size, color, materials, and proportions. A fly's *construction* is the method by which the thing is built. The Light Cahill and Hendrickson dry flies, for instance, are two different patterns. They're made of different materials and they represent two different bugs. But they are the same construction: If you can tie one, you can tie the other. Similarly, a 3-inch-long, white-and-chartreuse Lefty's Deceiver is not the same pattern as a 6-inch, yellow-and-red Deceiver—but these two flies are the same construction.

Nearly all of my nymphs share a common construction. Essentially a rip-off of the venerable Gold-Ribbed Hare's Ear, it's a design that cannot be improved by the likes of me. This style of nymph has neat tails, a segmented abdomen (with varying degrees of flash), a well-defined thorax, a pronounced wing case, either of two types of legs, and a tidy (though sometimes large) head. Those are the basic nymph parts. By varying the proportions, size, color, and materials, I can make this construction represent a small blue-winged olive nymph, a big brown-drake nymph, a black stonefly, a Hendrickson nymph, a damselfly nymph, a mayfly emerger, and lots of other insects. Or I can tie it my favorite way, as a generic mayfly larva with a flashy pearlescent rib.

Sure, there are other styles of nymphs, some of them quite elegant and others very realistic. But this simple construction made of inexpensive materials works as well as any other design.

Like most nymphs, those in this chapter have dubbed bodies. Unlike some, my nymphs have tight, neat bodies. Real mayfly larvae are exquisitely formed creatures, and I've never seen the point of tying loose, shaggy nymphs that look like wads of dryer lint stuck on hooks. I prefer flies that have clean, well-defined shapes, and the fish seem to agree. Besides, a tidy, tightly dubbed body lasts longer than a fat, loose one.

A knockoff of the venerable Gold-Ribbed Hare's Ear, this simple, versatile style of nymph can meet most requirements. Dubbing the body is the main challenge in tying a good nymph.

A NYMPH FOR ALL REASONS

Making those tight, neat bodies is the main challenge of tying these flies. Dubbing well is one of the most important fly-tying skills—in some ways, it's the essence of the craft—yet it's one that many tiers never master. Some tiers never become even halfway good at it. But if you can't make a tidy, sturdy, nicely shaped body with fur, you simply can't tie freshwater flies. So, we'll spend some time on the rudiments of dubbing in a little while. If you finish this chapter able to make a neat, durable nymph, you will have learned one of the most valuable lessons in the book—perhaps the most valuable.

First, though, let's look at the ingredients of nymphs.

THE PARTS

I use traditional, heavy-wire, 1X-long Sproat hooks such as the Mustad 3906B or Tiemco TMC 3761 for most nymphs from size 8 through size 16. Since they're made of substantial wire and have big gaps relative to the lengths of their shanks, these hooks weigh more than 2X- or 3X-long hooks of the same overall length. That's a good thing, since it reduces the amount of extra weight I need to add to a nymph.

If I want a nymph longer than a size 8, 1X-long hook, I'll go to a 2X-long iron such as a Mustad 9671 or Tiemco TMC 5262. That is, I'll use a 2X-long, size 8 hook rather than a 1X-long size 6. This decision has less to do with the weight of the hooks than with the appearance of flies tied on them. A fly tied on a size 6 Mustad 3906B has a big hunk of steel sticking out of its butt. While a fish might not recognize a hook as something dangerous, it might recognize a big gap and long point as something unnatural, something that doesn't belong on an insect. So, I use progressively longer-shank hooks for bigger nymphs. For jumbo stoneflies, hellgrammites, and other monster bugs, I'll use 3X-long hooks such as a Mustad 9672 or Tiemco TMC 5263.

Most mayfly nymphs can be tied on 1X-long hooks like the three in the center of the photo. For larger nymphs such as some mayflies and most stoneflies, 2X-long irons like those on the bottom work well. Standard-length wet-fly hooks like those on top are good chassis for very small nymphs.

When I need nymphs smaller than those I can tie on size 16, 1X-long hooks, I use standard-length wet-fly hooks. For instance, I'll tie an olive nymph on a size 16 Mustad 3906 (an old-fashioned wet-fly hook) rather than on a size 18 3906B (a 1X-long nymph hook). I can tie identical flies on those two hooks, but the 3906 weighs slightly more, and that's important on a tiny nymph that has practically no room for lead wire. The size 16 3906 also has a bigger gap and longer point than the size 18 3906B, and that can make a difference when I hook a fish.

For most mayfly-size nymphs, use 1X-long, heavy-wire hooks. When you want to tie a big nymph—a Green Drake, maybe, or a stonefly—use a 2X- or 3X-long model. Tie blue-winged olives and other wee nymphs on standard-length wet-fly hooks. In any case, pick a hook with a shank length appropriate for the bug you want the fly to represent.

Any reasonably fine thread will work for tying these nymphs. Brown, olive, and black are the three most useful colors.

Since most nymph patterns should sink quickly, most benefit from having some extra weight. "Some" is about all that will fit on a mayfly pattern. Wrapping the entire shank with weighting wire produces an overly fat foundation that makes for difficult tying and an ugly fly. Besides, an excessively heavy nymph has little movement in the water; it doesn't respond to currents the way a real nymph does. So, I weight my nymphs with two pieces of lead wire, each about two-thirds the length of the hook shank. One piece goes on each side of the hook. This method adds a little weight to the fly and produces a wide, flat foundation on which it's easy to build a nicely proportioned body. If I need more weight to get the fly down in deep or fast water, I add it to the leader. The sequential photos show how to weight a hook with two strips of wire.

Many tiers make the tails of a nymph with a little pinch of fur. That works well enough, but I prefer a small clump of hackle fibers; they look more like nymph tails. I use the same material to make legs on many nymphs.

Fine, oval, gold tinsel is the traditional rib material on nymphs, and it still works very well for making segments in the abdomen and adding a bit of sparkle to a fly. For a long time, though, I've been using pearlescent Krystal Flash as rib material on small to medium-size nymphs. Three pieces of Krystal Flash twisted into a rope and wrapped in a spiral over the abdomen add a color and a degree of glitter that trout seem to find very appealing. Maybe the sparkle of pearl Krystal Flash looks like the glint of tiny air bubbles, or maybe the stuff is simply more visible than gold tinsel. I don't have a good explanation—but I do know that nymphs ribbed with Krystal Flash catch fish very well.

The standard material for wing cases is a slip from a goose, duck, or turkey wing quill. Back when I lived in the New Jersey suburbs, where every pond and puddle is overrun with Canada geese that have forgotten how to migrate, I picked up dozens of goose quills every year. I still have some of them, and still use them to make wing cases on nymphs.

The only drawback of a quill-slip wing case is that it might split as you handle it. This problem is easily avoided by painting the vane of the feather with flexible cement. Let the cement dry, and then use a needle to split sections out of the quill.

These days, many tiers make wing cases with various plastic materials. I've even used electrician's tape to make wing cases on stoneflies. My favorite synthetic wing-case material is a Wapsi Fly product called Thin Skin. It's a stretchy plastic—

Inexpensive and widely available, rabbit strips can provide dubbing material in dozens of colors. Bunny fur is among the easiest dubbings to use.

some sort of vinyl, I assume—that comes on paper backing. It makes a handsome, durable wing case, and it comes in a raft of colors, including some mottled patterns. The tying sequence below shows a nymph made with a Thin Skin wing case.

I've left the body material for last because it is both the most important aspect of these flies and the hardest to explain. These nymphs have dubbed abdomens and thoraxes. In fly-tying usage, "dubbing" is both a noun and a verb. As a noun, it refers to material twisted onto the tying thread and then wrapped around the hook shank. Various animal furs are the oldest and most common dubbing materials, though many synthetic fibers and blends of fur and synthetics are also used. As a verb, the term refers to the act of applying the material to the thread. (I find it interesting that none of my dictionaries lists the fly-tying definition of "dubbing." Fly tiers have been using the term for centuries.)

Let's deal with dubbing as a noun first. The bodies of the nymphs in this chapter are made with fur—specifically, rabbit. Many other furs can be used, of course, but bunny fur is cheap, widely available in a huge range of colors, and very easy to use. The strips of rabbit hide used for tying Zonkers and many other flies are excellent sources of dubbing material. Zonker strips come in dozens of natural and dyed colors, which can be blended to produce even more colors and shades. With half a dozen packages of rabbit strips— tan, gray, black, olive, brown, and rust or dark orange—you can make dubbing for nearly any nymph or wet fly you will need for trout fishing.

Fly shops sell a great variety of packaged, blended, ready-to-use dubbings made of all sorts of natural and synthetic fibers. Most of these work more or less well, and you will no doubt find uses for many of them, as I have. But a fly tier should know how to make his own dubbing. Only by blending your own can you have complete control of the material's color, texture, and fiber length. Making your own also saves money. So let's make some.

PREPARING NYMPH DUBBING

You already have all the tools you need to make dubbing: scissors and fingers. But before you start chopping tufts of fur from a hide, take a minute to study the stuff. You will see that animal fur consists of two types of fibers. The shorter, softer, fuzzier, duller fibers are the under-fur. These are the fibers that stick to the thread; they are the "binder" that makes dubbing work. The longer, stiffer, shinier fibers are called guard hairs. They are what give a dubbed fly a shaggy, "spiky" appearance.

Nymph dubbings generally contain underfur and guard hairs, and are therefore easy to prepare—cut the fur from the hide and mix it all together. Sometimes, though, you want dubbing made only of underfur. Dry flies, for instance, typically have sleek, slender bodies, and dry-fly dubbing should consist only of underfur. Small nymphs often look better when made with dubbing that contains few or no guard hairs.

Separating guard hairs and underfur requires a little patience, but no great dexterity. Pinch a clump of fur near the tips, so

This strip of muskrat hide makes it easy to see the difference between underfur (the shorter, fuzzy material) and guard hairs (the longer, darker fibers). Some dubbings consist of both types of fibers; others use only the underfur. Most nymphs are made with dubbing that contains both underfur and guard hairs.

that you're holding all the guard hairs. With your other hand, use sharp, strong scissors to cut the fur as close to the hide as possible. Lift the tuft of fur from the hide and gently stroke the underfur out of the clump, leaving the guard hairs pinched between your thumb and forefinger. Discard the guard hairs. Of course, this is easier to do with some furs than with others. Muskrat is good fur to practice with, since it has long guard hairs. You can use the guard-hair-free (or "cleaned") dubbing for Adams and Dark Cahill dry flies.

For our nymphs, however, we'll use rabbit-fur dubbing that contains both underfur and guard hairs. It's easy to prepare, especially if you make it from Zonker strips. Put a sheet of clean paper on your desk. Cut the fur from about 3 inches of a Zonker strip and let it fall onto the paper. Snip the fur from the hide one clump at a time, and cut as close to the skin as you can.

Push all the fur on the paper into a pile. Just shove it all together—don't be gentle. Pick up the pile and pull it apart into two separate clumps. Put the two clumps back together, one on top of the other, and pull the new pile apart. Do it again. Keep shuffling the fur this way with your fingers until the underfur and guard hairs are mixed and jumbled, pointing in all directions.

That's all there is to it. While it doesn't lend itself to mass production, the shuffling method works with any material, natural or synthetic. You can use it to blend different colors, combining, for instance, brown and olive rabbit fur to make a brownish olive dubbing. Or you can mix different materi-

Blending fur by hand requires a little time and patience, but it doesn't demand any great skill. Simply pull a wad of fur into two clumps, put the clumps back together, pull the fur apart again, and so on. Essentially, you shuffle the fur until it is thoroughly mixed.

als—blending, say, two parts of bunny fur with one part of fine Antron fibers to make a soft, slightly glittery dubbing for caddis pupa patterns.

Blending fur by hand—or "dry blending," as it's sometimes called—has the drawback of producing only a little dubbing material at a time. People who need to make large amounts of dubbing, such as materials suppliers or commercial fly tiers, use other methods to blend fur. But shuffling the stuff by hand will produce more than enough material for an amateur tier's needs. It's how I prepare all my dubbings, and I tie a few flies.

Some tiers use small blenders or food processors or even coffee grinders to blend fur. Power blending certainly mixes the material, but it also chops most of the fibers into short pieces, and for that reason I don't like it. Dubbing made up of very short fibers tends to produce rougher, shaggier flies. I prefer hand-blended fur, and recommend it to you.

The act of twisting fur onto thread is, for my money, the skill that defines this craft. Knowing how to dub lets you turn a few inches of tying thread into body material. Knowing how to dub well lets you turn pieces of animal hides and wads of synthetic fibers into an infinite variety of fly bodies. If you've had trouble with this aspect of fly tying—and nearly everyone has—you might find the next section helpful.

TYING TIPS

Nymphs are smaller than the flies we've tied in previous chapters, but they're not very difficult as long as you can handle dubbing reasonably well. If you're a novice or if you simply have trouble with dubbing, devote a little time and 50 cents' worth of material to practicing the technique. Trying to learn how to dub while also trying to tie an unfamiliar fly makes no sense. Master the basic skill first, and then apply it to a pattern. This approach helps as much with dubbing as it does with deer hair.

Most problems with dubbing stem from using too much material. I believe it was Ed Engle, a fine fly tier and fly-tying author, who quoted a fellow tier as saying that he used just enough dubbing "to dirty the thread." That's a good way to think of it. With a little practice, you will be able to manage a heavier load of dubbing on the thread. At first, though, apply small, tiny, minute, minuscule, itty-bitty amounts of fur to the thread, particularly when tying trout flies. Start with a wisp of material that looks ridiculously sparse, and then use only half of that.

What if you want to build a thick, tapered body? Do it by wrapping multiple layers of dubbed thread. Yes, it takes a little extra time. But dubbing a body in layers gives you perfect control over its thickness and shape, and always produces a better-looking, more durable fly.

You apply dubbing to thread by rolling the material and the thread between the tips of your thumb and index finger. Fly tiers generally use the term "twisting" for this operation. Roll—or twist—in one direction only, not back and forth. For instance, I roll dubbing onto thread by sliding my thumb toward the tip of my index finger. Then I let go, get a fresh grip on the material and thread, and roll again in the same direction.

Some tiers use wax when they dub, some don't. I can't remember the last time I used dubbing wax. Novices, however, often find that a little extra wax on the thread helps the fur to stick. If you use wax (but I recommend that you don't), pass it along the thread *once*. Do not slather a thick coat of sticky wax on your tying thread; too much wax robs dubbing material of its color, luster, and fuzzy texture. That's why I never use the stuff.

Let's roll through the rudiments once.

THE RUDIMENTS OF DUBBING

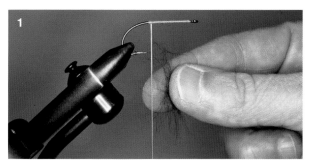

Clamp any old big hook in your vise. Wrap a base of thread on the hook; to make the photography easier, I'm using relatively heavy thread here. Tease a wisp of dubbing out of the main clump. And I do mean a wisp—note how little material is between my fingertips. Always remember the three primary rules of dubbing: Use less material; use less material; use less material. This material is rabbit, though it could be nearly any soft fur.

Cradle the bobbin in your left hand. Hold the wisp of material against the thread. Roll the thread and fur between your fingertips. Roll in one direction only. Here, I'm sliding my thumb toward the tip of my index finger. Then I'll let go, get a fresh grip, and roll the material in the same direction again. Never twist dubbing back and forth between your fingertips.

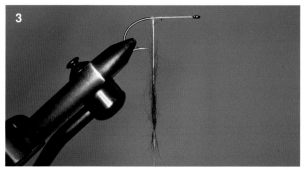

Roll the material two or three times—just enough so that it stays in place on the thread. We'll twist it more tightly in a minute.

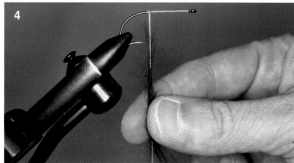

Tease another wisp of dubbing from the big clump and add it below the first wisp. Roll the material and thread between your thumb and forefinger two or three times, twisting it just enough so that it stays in place on the thread. Remember to twist in only one direction. Add a third wisp of dubbing below the second one.

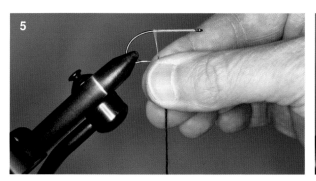

Now twist all the dubbing tightly. Don't pull the thread too tight as you do this; hold the bobbin gently in your left hand and keep the thread just barely taut. Squeeze hard as you roll the thread and fur between your thumb and the tips of your first two fingers. After you've been tying dubbed flies for a while, the thumb muscles on your right hand will be noticeably larger than those on your left.

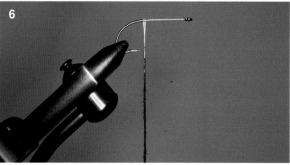

Here's what you want to produce: a neat, thin layer of fur on the thread. Note that, in places, the thread is visible through the dubbing. You don't always have to dub this sparsely, but you will avoid most problems if you do.

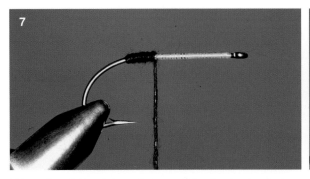

Wrap the dubbed thread around the hook shank. Lay each turn against the previous one. This is how we build bodies on most trout flies that represent insects.

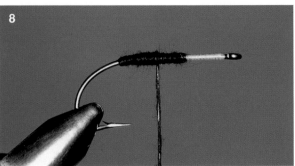

To make a thicker or tapered body, wrap several layers of dubbed thread. Add material to the thread as necessary.

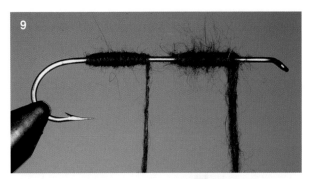

Here's a comparison of sparse and heavy dubbing—same thread, same material. The body on the left, formed by wrapping several layers of lightly dubbed thread, is tight and neat. The body on the right was made with one layer of heavily dubbed thread. It's looser and shaggier, and it would prove considerably less durable in the field. Try to make bodies like the example on the left.

You can make a nymph more durable by dubbing a tiny bit of the abdomen before attaching the rib material. Twist a very small wisp of fur onto the thread, and wrap a little ball of dubbing at the base of the tails. Then tie in the rib material, dub the rest of the abdomen, and wind the rib forward. The little ball of dubbing behind the first turn of rib will keep it from sliding off the rear of the body as fish chew on the fly.

Real nymphs come in many sizes and shapes, which means that fake nymphs don't have fixed proportions. In general, though, make a nymph's tails not quite as long as the hook shank. The abdomen should fill half to two-thirds of the hook shank, and the thorax and head should fill the rest. Try to give the abdomen a tapered shape, and make the thorax fatter than the rest of the body. Hackle-fiber legs should be slightly shorter than the fibers used for the tails. Use a wing case broad enough to cover the top of the thorax, and don't worry about making an itty-bitty head; most real nymphs have substantial heads.

Enough abstractions. Let's build an example.

TYING AN ALL-AROUND NYMPH

I've caught hundreds of trout with flies like the one we're about to tie. There's nothing radical or original about it, and it doesn't represent any single species of mayfly, but it bears a rough resemblance to many nymphs and will take fish in every season. I've never had a name for it, but I guess it needs one now. Let's call it a Pearl Bunny Nymph. Here's the recipe.

Hook: 1X-long, heavy-wire nymph hook, size 12.

Thread: Brown.

Weight (optional, but recommended): A strip of lead wire lashed to each side of the hook shank.

Tails: Brown hackle fibers.

Abdomen: Natural grayish tan (or tannish gray) rabbit fur.

Rib: Three pieces of pearlescent Krystal Flash twisted together.

Wing case: A section from a goose quill that has been treated with flexible cement.

Thorax: The same dubbing used for the abdomen.

Legs: A few brown hackle fibers tied on each side of the hook.

Preparing a Goose Quill

Start by preparing some wing-case material. If you want to use a piece of goose, duck, or turkey quill, paint the shiny side of the feather—the side that faced in when the quill was still on the bird—with flexible cement. Flexament or vinyl cement works well. Don't use lacquer or nail polish. Set the quill aside to dry. This is a goose quill that has already contributed a number of wing cases to nymphs.

Weight and Tails

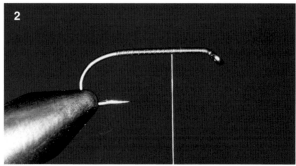

Put a nymph hook (this is a Mustad 3906B) in your vise and wrap a base of thread on it. Wind back to the end of the shank and then forward to a spot about one-third of the way behind the eye.

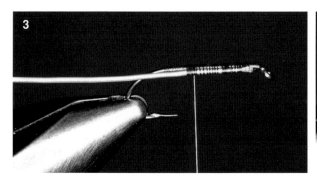

Cut a piece of weighting wire about 2 inches long. Use wire that's no thicker than the hook wire. Bind the wire along one side of the shank. Leave a little space between the end of the wire and the hook eye. Don't bind the wire all the way to the end of the shank; you will want a little space at the aft end, too. Bind the weight tightly to the hook.

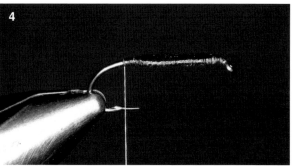

Cut the wire or break it by wiggling it back and forth. Repeat the operation on the other side of the shank. Make sure that both pieces of weight are even with the hook shank, then apply cement to the wraps and wind one more layer of thread, finishing at the rear of the hook. The hook is now not only weighted, but also ready to serve as a wide foundation for the body of your nymph.

A b d o m e n   a n d   R i b

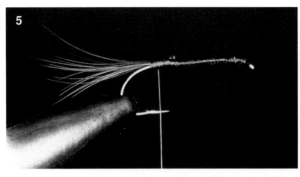

Cut or strip a few fibers from a brown hackle feather. Tie them in at the hook bend. This operation is much like attaching the wing to a bucktail (see chapter 4), but in miniature. Trim the tail butts and bind them down.

Twist a tiny amount of dubbing onto the thread and wrap a little ball of fur at the base of the tails. Note how little material is on the thread.

Here's the little ball of dubbing. This trick simplifies making the first wrap with the rib and pretty much eliminates the rib's tendency to slide off the end of the abdomen, which, of course, makes for a longer-lasting fly.

Traditionally, nymphs have ribs made with tinsel or wire. This fly will have a rib made of pearlescent Krystal Flash. Cut three pieces of Krystal Flash about 3 inches long (four pieces on a big nymph). Attach the material right in front of the little ball of dubbing. Bind down the ends.

Twist a thin, tight layer of fur on the thread. Begin wrapping the abdomen. Wrap several layers of dubbed thread to build up the abdomen and give it a taper, adding material to the thread as necessary.

The abdomen should cover slightly more than half of the hook shank and taper toward the tails. This is best accomplished by wrapping several thin layers of dubbing. Leave plenty of room for the thorax and head.

Grab the Krystal Flash with your hackle pliers. Twist the material six or eight times to make a flashy rope. Wind the Krystal Flash rope in a spiral over the abdomen. This is a size 8 fly, so the abdomen gets six turns of rib. A size 12 or 14 fly needs only four or at most five turns.

Tie down the Krystal Flash at the front of the abdomen. To do this, hold the rib taut with your right hand and pass the bobbin over the hook with your left. Make five or six wraps of thread this way. You can then let go of the Krystal Flash, trim the excess, and bind down the stubs.

Thorax, Wing Case, and Legs

Use a needle to split a section out of your cemented wing quill. This quill section should be wide enough to cover the top of the nymph's thorax; make it at least as wide at the fattest part of the abdomen. Cut the section from the feather.

Attach the quill section against the front of the abdomen. The shiny side (the side you painted with flexible cement) goes up. Bind the material tightly in place.

Twist some fur on the thread and dub the nymph's thorax. Make the thorax slightly fatter than the abdomen; a nymph should have a buxom, chesty figure. Don't crowd the hook eye—you need room for several more steps.

Let's give this nymph hackle-fiber legs. Cut or strip a few fibers from a brown hackle. Hold them against one side of the hook at the front of the thorax and tie them in place. Attach a few more fibers on the other side of the hook. Then carefully trim the butts and bind them down.

Pull the quill segment over the top of the thorax to make the wing case. Bind it down at the front. Make several tight wraps of thread, and then clip the excess quill segment.

Wrap a neat head—you won't have to make many wraps—and whip-finish the thread. Don't worry about making a tiny head; real nymphs have fairly large noggins. Give the head two coats of cement or lacquer.

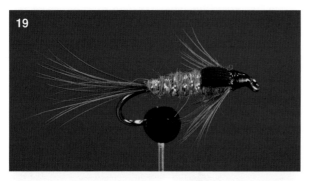

Here's the same fly in more natural light. It has all the essential nymph components, a good shape, and a rib that gives off subtle glints of light. In sizes 12 and 14, this pattern is one of the most reliable flies a trout fisherman can have.

A PLASTIC WING CASE AND PICKED-OUT LEGS

Hackle-fiber legs look great, but they can be tricky to add to a small nymph. And I'm not sure that they make a difference on a size 14 or smaller fly. Besides, it's easier and quicker to make the legs by picking out some of the fur on the thorax. That's the traditional method on the Gold-Ribbed Hare's Ear, and it works beautifully with many types of fur.

Let's give this next nymph a synthetic wing case made with a material called Thin Skin, an excellent product from Wapsi Fly. It comes in scads of solid and mottled colors; we'll use a color called "mottled oak," which has a pattern like that of a wing feather from a wild turkey. We'll also give this fly a traditional gold rib. The thread, tails, and dubbing are the same as on the Pearl Bunny Nymph.

Weight the hook and construct the tails as you did on the previous fly. Wrap a tiny ball of dubbing at the base of the tails, and then attach a piece of fine oval tinsel. Dub the abdomen and wind the rib.

Thin Skin comes on a paper backing, which makes the material easier to trim to size. Cut a strip wide enough to cover the top of the fly. Trim one end to a steep point.

Peel the Thin Skin off the paper backing. Attach the pointed end to the hook. You will see that the material has one shiny side and one dull side. Fish don't seem to care which side shows on the finished fly; I generally attach Thin Skin so that the shiny side will show when the fly is done.

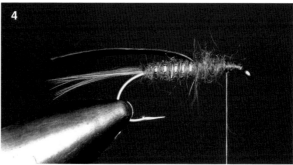

Dub a fat thorax. Don't try to do this by twisting huge wads of fur onto the thread; that approach will produce a fly that quickly falls apart. Use a moderate amount of fur, twist it tightly onto the thread, and build the thorax by wrapping five or six layers.

Pull the Thin Skin over the top of the thorax and tie it down. Make several tight wraps of thread, cut off the excess Thin Skin, and bind down the stub.

Build up the head and whip-finish the thread. Again, don't worry about making an itty-bitty head.

With a needle, ideally a dull one, gently pick at the sides of the thorax to tease out some of the dubbing fibers. After picking out the legs, give the head two coats of cement or lacquer. This construction is just like the classic Gold-Ribbed Hare's Ear, but with Thin Skin in place of a quill segment. The legs grow out of the thorax, just as a real nymph's do. As an all-around trout fly, this nymph is hard to beat.

OPTIONS AND VARIATIONS

With an assortment of rabbit fur and feathers, you can make our simple nymph construction represent almost any mayfly larva and even some stoneflies. If you want to make precise matches of specific insects, you'll have to collect some from the streams you fish. Or you can study patterns and photos in fly-tying books and magazines and then replicate them as well as possible with the materials that you have. Worry most about size and color, and don't fret too much over materials. If you read about a good-looking pattern dubbed with fur from the inner left thigh of a virgin wombat, don't make yourself crazy trying to find exactly that material. Blend some rabbit fur until you have dubbing that's roughly the right color, tie some flies, and go catch fish.

Tie some nymphs to match the water, too. Mayfly nymphs that live in fast, choppy water are generally short, squat, and flattened; they have relatively long tails and muscular legs. Adjust the proportions of our all-purpose bunny-fur nymph, giving it slightly longer tails and a slightly shorter abdomen, and you'll have a fine fly for fast freestone brooks. Burrowing nymphs that live in slower water typically have long, slender abdomens and short tails; their tails are sometimes broad and fringed. But with some adjustments, our bunny-fur nymph will work again. Use a 2X-long hook, make the tails with fluffy fibers from the base of a saddle feather, and dub a long abdomen.

Pay attention to the color of the riverbed. Prey creatures tend to match their surroundings. If the bottom consists mostly of tan and brown stones and gravel, use a tannish brown nymph. A stream with a dark bottom probably contains darker nymphs; try one made with black thread, dark grizzly tails and legs, and gray squirrel or muskrat dubbing.

It's heresy to say this, but you don't have to be a good entomologist to tie good nymphs. Pay attention to the habitat, take note of any bugs you see, and turn over a few rocks now and then. If you do those things, you can catch a lot of trout.

Here are a handful of patterns all built with the techniques you've already learned. You can tie them weighted or unweighted, except for the Easy Stonefly, which should always be weighted.

Early Season Nymph

This fly is essentially a Gold-Ribbed Hare's Ear with tails and legs made with fibers from a wood duck flank feather. I've had good luck with it early in the season, from the Quill Gordon through the Hendrickson hatches, and even during the light Cahill hatch, which comes a little later.

Hook: Heavy wire, 1X long, sizes 12 and 14.
Thread: Brown or reddish brown.
Tails: Wood duck fibers nearly as long as the hook shank.
Abdomen: Natural rabbit fur.
Rib: Fine oval or flat gold tinsel.
Wing case: Dark goose-quill section.
Thorax: Natural rabbit fur.
Legs: Wood duck fibers.

Squirrel Nymphs

These are good year-round flies in streams with dark bottoms. They also work well before and during hatches of dark mayflies. I tie them in two versions, one with a Krystal Flash rib and the other with a rib of heavy black thread. The darker version with the black rib seems a little more effective in slow water. Trout don't seem to care whether the tails and legs are made with teal-flank fibers or grizzly hackle fibers, or whether the wing case is a piece of goose quill or a strip of Thin Skin.

As its name indicates, an Early Season Nymph is a good choice in April, May, and part of June. Although it's not a perfect match for any specific insect, this pattern suggests a number of mayflies that emerge early in the trout season.

Squirrel Nymphs work particularly well in dark-bottomed streams. They can be tied with a variety of materials, but the bodies are always gray squirrel fur.

Hook: Heavy wire, 1X long, sizes 10 through 16.
Thread: Black.
Tails: Dark grizzly hackle fibers or teal-flank fibers.
Abdomen: Gray squirrel body fur.
Rib: Three or four pieces of pearlescent Krystal Flash twisted into a rope, or heavy black thread (rod-winding thread works well).
Wing case: Dark goose-quill section or mottled-oak Thin Skin.
Thorax: Gray squirrel body fur.
Legs: Dark grizzly hackle fibers or teal-flank fibers.

A NYMPH FOR ALL REASONS

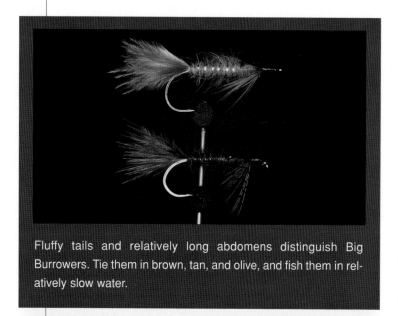

Fluffy tails and relatively long abdomens distinguish Big Burrowers. Tie them in brown, tan, and olive, and fish them in relatively slow water.

Since they're small, olive nymphs are best tied on standard-length wet-fly hooks. These little guys can come in handy several times during a season, since many rivers have more than one hatch of blue-winged olives and similar mayflies.

Big Burrowers

Use these in slow water with a soft bottom or during the drake hatches (brown, yellow, and green) in June and July. The fluffy tails have lots of movement in slow water and resemble the fringed appendages of some large mayfly nymphs. Slow-water nymphs also have prominent gills, which you can approximate by brushing the abdomen to make it slightly fuzzy. A stiff toothbrush or a .22-caliber bore-cleaning brush works well for this operation.

Hook: 2X long, sizes 8 through 12.
Thread: Brown or olive.
Tails: A few fluffy fibers from the base of a brown, tan, or olive saddle hackle.
Abdomen: Brown, tan, or olive rabbit fur. Make the abdomen occupy at least two-thirds of the hook shank. Muddy olive—a mix of brown, natural, and olive fur—is a good color for brown drake and green drake nymphs. For yellow drake nymphs, natural tan fur usually works well enough.
Rib: Gold oval tinsel or copper wire.
Wing case: Mottled-oak Thin Skin.
Thorax: Brown, tan, or olive rabbit fur.
Legs: Fibers from a brown, tan, or olive feather. Saddle hackles, hen hackles, partridge feathers, and grouse feathers are all good.

Olives

Since most olive mayflies are small, I generally tie these nymphs on standard-length wet-fly hooks. A size 16 wet-fly hook is very nearly the same length as a size 18 1X-long nymph hook, but the former weighs a little more and has a bigger gap. It's your call, but I think that you'll find that small nymphs tied on wet-fly hooks sink a little better and hold fish more securely.

"Olive" is a broad term, but *Baetis* and other olive nymphs vary in color in from place to place. Generally, though, a blend of olive and brown rabbit fur works well enough on a nymph pattern. Some olive mayflies are quite dark; add a little black fur to the mix to tie darker nymphs. Because these are small flies, you might want to prepare a batch of dubbing that has very few guard hairs. Dubbing that contains relatively few guard hairs is easier to use when tying small patterns.

Hook: Standard wet-fly hook, sizes 14 and 16, or 1X-long nymph hook, sizes 16 and 18.

Thread: Olive or dark olive.

Tails: Dark dun, olive grizzly, or dyed-olive partridge fibers. Dyed partridge makes lovely tails, though it's not easy to find. Make the tails as long as the hook shank.

Abdomen: Olive rabbit fur.

Rib: Copper wire or brown thread.

Wing case: Dark goose-quill section or mottled-oak Thin Skin.

Thorax: Olive rabbit fur.

Legs: The same hackle fibers used for the tails, or picked-out fur as on a Hare's Ear.

Early Stonefly

Many trout streams have a hatch of small, slender black stoneflies in late winter or early spring, before the mayfly action begins. Unlike most of their relatives that crawl out of the water to emerge, the little black stoneflies hatch in the surface film. I've run into this hatch on sunny, late-winter days and enjoyed some good fishing with a black nymph cast on a greased leader and drifted about a foot below the surface.

Hook: 2X long, sizes 10 and 12.

Thread: Black.

Tails: Black hackle fibers.

Abdomen: Black rabbit fur. Make the abdomen and thorax fairly slender; these are thin insects.

Rib: Black rod-winding thread.

Wing case: Black Thin Skin, a black goose-quill section, or even a narrow strip of electrician's tape.

Thorax: Black rabbit fur.

Legs: Black hackle fibers or fur picked out from the thorax.

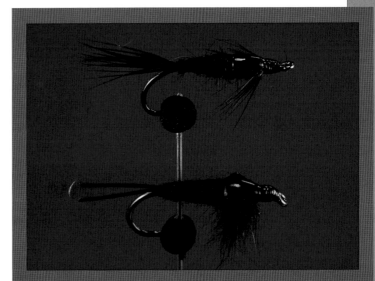

The Early Stonefly (top) and Easy Stonefly will take trout in most freestone streams. They're constructed just like the mayfly nymphs.

Easy Stonefly

Most healthy freestone streams contain at least one type of black stonefly that emerges during the summer. These insects can take two years to mature, which means that trout see and eat the nymphs all year, and that makes a black nymph a good choice whenever you don't know what to fish. Although you will probably graduate to more complex, sophisticated patterns, you will find that this simple fly does a more-than-adequate job of representing an immature stonefly nymph. It's particularly good in fast water with a rocky bottom and in the head of a pool. Unlike most of the larger stonefly patterns that mimic mature nymphs, this one is pleasant to cast with a light line.

Hook: 2X long, sizes 8 through 12.
Thread: Black.
Weight: Heavy lead wire on both sides of the hook shank.
Tails: Fine rubber material.
Abdomen: Black rabbit fur.
Rib: Black rod-winding thread.
Wing case: Black Thin Skin, a black goose-quill section,
or a narrow strip of electrician's tape.
Thorax: Black rabbit fur.
Legs: Black hackle fibers or fur picked out from the thorax.

Foamback Emerger

With two important changes, the simple Pearl Bunny construction makes a very good emerger. Since you want the fly to hang in the surface film, substitute a light-wire dry-fly hook for the usual nymph iron. For the wing case, use a narrow strip of closed-cell foam, which functions as a tiny float on top of the fly. This sort of fly isn't the easiest to see on the water, but fish love it. It's not restricted to the very beginning of a hatch; indeed, a Foamback will usually catch fish through an entire emergence.

You can tie these in sizes and colors to match whatever mayflies you expect to see. The following pattern doesn't represent anything in particular, but it has caught fish for me from early April until well into June, covering hatches matched with flies as different as Quill Gordons and Light Cahills. Fish it with a 5X or 6X tippet.

A dry-fly hook and a strip of closed-cell foam turn a nymph into an emerger pattern.

Hook: Standard dry fly, sizes 10 to 16.
Thread: Brown or reddish brown.
Tails: Brown or ginger hackle fibers.
Abdomen: Natural rabbit fur.
Rib: Three strands of pearlescent Krystal Flash twisted together.
Wing case: A strip of brown closed-cell foam. After tying down the foam at the front of the thorax, cut it square at the rear edge of the hook eye.
Thorax: Natural rabbit fur.
Legs: Brown or ginger hackle fibers, or picked-out fur.

They're all different, and yet all pretty much the same, at least in method of construction. Vary colors and proportions, and sometimes materials, and you can make scores of different nymphs that are all built the same way. Just remember to go easy with the dubbing material—use less, use less, use less—and you will have no trouble tying beautiful nymphs for all reasons.

Hardly a year passes without one of the fly-fishing magazines running an article about forgotten, neglected, overlooked, or out-of-fashion wet flies. Besides lamenting the diminished popularity of old-fashioned wet-fly angling, these articles share the stunning revelation that these patterns will catch hip, up-to-date trout.

Of course they will. Wet flies were fooling trout back when Dame Juliana Berners was still playing with dolls. Unless we wreck all of our rivers, they will be fooling trout centuries hence. And yet each year-class of contemporary anglers seems to discover wet flies with all the amazement and joy of teenagers discovering sex. Both are lots of fun to watch.

Wet flies come in many varieties, and they work because they imitate or suggest a great many types of fish food. Some of the old, tinsel-bodied patterns such as the Butcher probably mimic tiny fry. Others, such as the elegant Parmachenee (or Parmacheene) Belle, are simply good lures. No doubt the wet versions of the Dark Cahill, March Brown, and many other patterns can represent mayflies that failed at emergence. Quite a few wet flies are just buggy-looking things that trout figure they might as well eat. And many simple wet flies imitate caddis pupae, caddis emergers, or diving, egg-laying caddis.

It's those last two groups—buggy-looking things and underwater caddis—on which I want to concentrate. Both catch fish in most streams and for most of the trout season; neither requires a lot of skill to tie. Depending on how it's fished, a bare-bones wet fly consisting of only a body and a swept-back hackle makes an adequate imitation of a caddis pupa drifting in the current, a mature pupa rising toward the surface to emerge, or an adult female caddis that has returned to the water to lay eggs. Add a tail to that simple construction, and you have a lure that can suggest a mayfly nymph or an emerger.

Simple, two-part wet flies can represent caddis pupae and egg-laying female caddis, and they'll catch trout anywhere. The fly on the left has a muskrat-fur body. The one on the right has a body dubbed with a blend of olive fur and green Antron, and a dyed-olive partridge hackle.

These are very old styles of flies. An angler from the 1500s would recognize them and wouldn't need any instructions from us on how to fish them. These days, the body-and-collar variety is most often called a soft-hackle wet fly, though the term is sometimes used loosely. A fly that has a tail as well as a dubbed body and a hackle belongs to a group often called flymphs, a term coined many years ago by an angler named Pete Hidy.

Although these are simple flies, their hackle collars give some tiers fits. A proper wet-fly collar lies back at a rakish angle, with the fibers evenly distributed around the hook and free to move in the current. I struggled with wet-fly hackles for years, until I learned a good method for making a sparse, neat, angled collar. We'll look at this method in a few minutes, after a glance at the few parts of these simple, graceful flies.

THE PARTS

Traditional wet-fly hooks are made of relatively heavy wire. They typically have Sproat bends, turned-down eyes, and shanks a tiny bit shorter than those of standard dry-fly hooks. The Mustad 3906 is probably the best-known example.

A turned-down eye was necessary years ago, when wet flies were either tied with snells or attached to gut leaders by means of Turle knots. These days, a down-eye hook has few (if any) advantages, and a straight-eye hook makes a perfectly good chassis for a modern wet fly. About a third of my wets are tied on traditional down-eye hooks—I simply like how they look—and about a third are built on straight-eye Mustad 3366 hooks. Fish do not seem to have a preference.

The final third of my wet flies are tied on 1X-long nymph hooks. Some patterns look better or more nicely balanced on these hooks. Anything that might be mistaken for a mayfly nymph or emerger benefits from the extra length of a Mustad 3906B, Tiemco TMC 3761, or similar hook.

Wet flies have no special thread requirements. Flymaster 6/0, size 8/0 Uni-Thread or Gudebrod thread, 70-denier Ultra Thread, and equivalent products all work fine.

Wet-fly bodies are made with a number of materials. The traditional soft-hackle patterns have bodies consisting of a layer or two of silk floss or thread. Wet flies made with peacock herl have been around for centuries. Some wets have shiny tinsel bodies. Rabbit, muskrat, Australian possum, fox, and most other types of dubbing, including various synthetics, make lovely wet-fly bodies. We'll tie one type of wet with a herl body, and another that has a body dubbed with a blend of bunny fur and fine Antron.

Which sort of feather to use for the hackle depends on the effect you want to achieve and the type of water in which you will use the fly. Body feathers from partridges, grouse, and other gamebirds have soft, speckled fibers that make beautiful hackles with lots of movement. But these feathers, the true soft hackles, can lie all the way back over the body, forming a kind of sheath, when a fly is fished on a tight line in a moderate or fast current. That's fine if it's the effect that you want; a fly with a pressed-back hackle surrounding the body looks a lot like a caddis pupa. In slow water, or if you're tossing the fly upstream and fishing it on a dead drift, a soft partridge or grouse hackle keeps its shape and has excellent action.

If you want a slightly stiffer hackle, use a feather from a hen neck. A hen hackle has good action, but it's somewhat less likely than a partridge feather to collapse along the fly's body. Hen-neck feathers come in dozens of natural and dyed colors, and they make good all-around hackles on wet flies.

Some tiers use hen-back or hen-saddle feathers to hackle wet flies, but I'm not crazy about the results. A hen-back feather typically has so much web—the tiny barbules that allow the fibers to zip together when a bird preens its feathers—that the fibers don't want to separate as I wrap the hackle. I'd rather use a partridge or grouse feather; it makes a prettier fly.

Some wet-fly experts use feathers from inexpensive Indian or Chinese rooster necks on flies intended for fishing in fast water. These relatively stiff cock hackles, they argue, will vibrate in strong currents, yet still keep their shape. Note that these chaps are referring to imported, low-grade rooster hackles, and not to premium dry-fly feathers from specially bred birds.

It's fun to split hairs, but hen hackles or gamebird feathers will work fine on most wet flies. With some partridge feathers and brown, grizzly, black, and gray hen necks, a tier can make pretty nearly any wet fly he needs to catch fish.

TYING TIPS

Conventional wisdom holds that a dubbed wet-fly body should be rougher and shaggier than a dry-fly body made with fur. That's generally true, but it doesn't mean that you should dub a loose, fat, sloppy body. Even if you want a rough or fuzzy fly, don't try to make the body with a single layer of dubbing. Twist a thin, neat layer of material onto the tying thread, and form the body by wrapping two or more layers of dubbed thread. To make the body shaggy, tease it with a small, stiff brush. If you do it this way, the body will both look great and hold up through many attacks by fish.

The thickness of a wet fly's body depends on the type of bug the pattern is supposed to resemble. To make the relatively plump abdomen of a caddis, wrap several layers of dubbing and tease the body with a brush. Give a mayfly pattern a more slender body.

The main tying challenge, of course, is the conical hackle. Merely wrapping a feather around the hook won't produce it. The feather has to be folded and manipulated so that all the fibers lean toward the rear of the fly. Many tiers fold a feather—that is, force all of the fibers to the same side of the stem—before attaching it to a hook. But the best method I've found is one taught to me by Davy Wotton, a extraordinarily skilled fly tier from Wales. Davy folds a wet fly's hackle after attaching its tip end to the hook, and he continues to fold and manipulate the feather as he wraps it. His method works with any feather, and it took the headaches out of wet-fly tying for me. It also lets me make better collars on such streamer patterns as Zonkers and Matukas.

To make the photos a little easier to shoot and considerably easier to understand, I used a big hook and a large saddle hackle in the following demonstration. A novice wet-fly tier or someone who has struggled with these hackles might find it helpful to practice with similarly large components. The technique works just as well on trout-size hooks.

Wrapping a Wet–Fly Collar

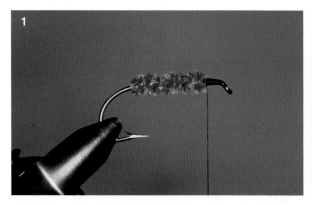

We'll make a simple fly, just a body and a hackle. On this size 2 hook, I used chenille for the body. On a trout fly, of course, you will probably use dubbing or peacock herl. When you finish the body, leave a smidgen of extra space in the head area of the fly; the hackle will use up the extra room.

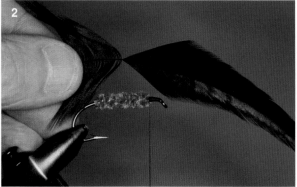

Strip the fluff from the butt end of the hackle feather. Stroke some of the fibers toward the butt, separating them from the rest of the fibers. You will use only enough of the feather to make two or three wraps of hackle.

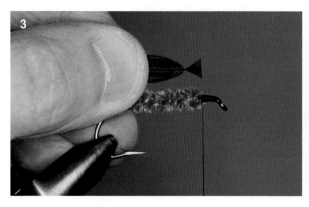

Hold the stroked-back fibers between your thumb and forefinger. Cut off the rest of the feather, leaving a triangular stub like this.

Tie the triangular stub to the bottom or side of the hook shank. The convex side of the feather faces out; the dull, concave side is toward the hook.

Lift the feather upright. A small feather with a short section of stripped stem is easier to handle with hackle pliers than with your fingers. With a big feather or one that has a long piece of stripped stem, just use your fingers. Note that the fibers are roughly parallel with the hook shank; half point forward, and the other half rearward.

Begin folding the feather by stroking the forward-pointing fibers around the far side of the hackle stem and pulling them toward the rear. With most feathers, you'll have to repeat the operation two or three times, stroking and pinching the fibers to force them toward the rear of the hook.

Hold on to the folded section of the feather as you begin the first wrap. Naturally, you'll have to let go of the fibers to bring the feather under the hook. As you finish the first full wrap, stroke all the fibers rearward again.

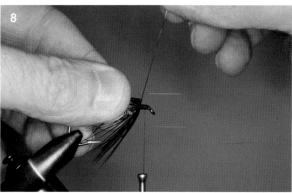

Make another wrap with the folded feather. The second turn of hackle should be in front of the first one; don't make the second wrap on top of the first one. As you finish the second wrap, stroke the fibers rearward again. In effect, you're folding the feather as you go. On many flies, particularly small patterns, two turns of hackle are enough. This feather can make about half a turn more, so let's use it.

Secure the stem of the hackle feather. Note how all the fibers lie at an angle, forming a cone. This is how a wet-fly hackle should look. A trout fly, of course, generally has a sparser hackle than this.

On most trout flies, two to three wraps of hackle are enough. Tiers who favor sparse flies will use a single turn of hackle or strip the fibers from one side of the feather before attaching it to the hook. A stripped feather doesn't require folding, and that makes the job a little easier. Generally, though, two wraps of a folded hen-neck feather will produce a good collar.

The length of a wet fly's hackle varies according to the style and purpose of the pattern. A flymph that represents a mayfly might have a hackle with fibers just long enough to reach the point of the hook. When it's pressed back by the current, the sparse collar of a soft-hackle caddis extends to at least the end of the body. Some old wet flies called Spiders have hackles that reach beyond the bends of their hooks.

If you have trouble making a wet-fly collar, practice with big hooks and large feathers. Once you get the hang of folding and wrapping a hackle, you can tie a bunch of simple, handsome, effective wet flies. You'll also have a skill that you will use on some streamer flies and many patterns for salmon and steelhead.

TYING A GRAY HACKLE, PEACOCK

You can tie this old pattern with or without a red tail. Without a tail, it must look like some sort of caddisfly to the trout. With the tail, it doesn't look much like anything a trout eats—yet the standard, tailed version of the fly catches fish very well. So does a red-and-white Dardevle spoon, of course. Some things are simply good lures.

I've included this fly for a reason besides utility. It has a peacock-herl body. Peacock is a common material with loads of fish appeal, but it's also fragile. We'll tie the Gray Hackle, Peacock with an unusual method that reinforces the frail quill of the peacock herl by counterwinding the tying thread through it. This trick works on many other peacock-bodied flies.

Here's the traditional recipe.

Hook: Standard-length wet fly, sizes 10 through 16.
Thread: Black.
Tail: Red hackle fibers.
Body: Peacock herl.
Hackle: Grizzly hen feather.

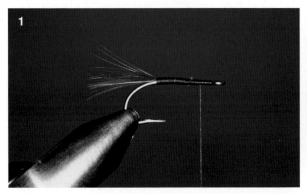

Wrap a base of thread on the hook. Tie on a small clump of red hackle fibers and bind down their butts. Advance the thread to the head area of the shank, leaving a little extra room so that you can wrap the hackle collar later.

Attach the butt ends of two pieces of peacock herl. The herl can point forward, as shown, or angle off the far side of the hook shank. Wind the thread rearward to the base of the tails.

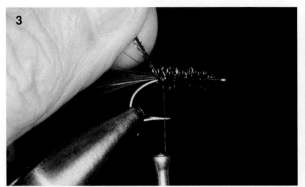

Wrap the two strands of herl rearward. You will probably find it easier to use your fingers rather than hackle pliers. When you reach the rear of the shank, where the thread is hanging, hold the herl taut and make one tight wrap of the thread, pinning the stems of the herl against the hook.

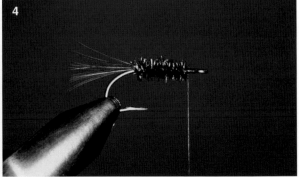

Keep the thread tight as you spiral it forward through the herl body. The thread pretty much disappears in the peacock herl, but it helps reinforce the extremely fragile stems. With the very tips of your scissors, clip the leftover herl at the rear of the hook.

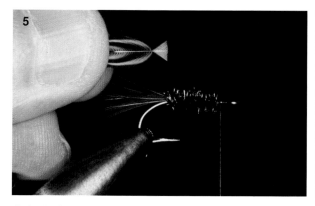

Strip the base of a grizzly hen hackle. Stroke some of the fibers—enough for about two turns of hackle—toward the butt of the feather. Cut off the tip end, leaving a triangular stub.

Tie the triangular stub to the hook. Elevate the feather and begin folding it as shown earlier. This feather has been folded once; it needs at least one more treatment.

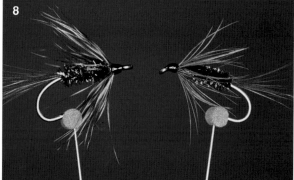

Make two turns of hackle. Stroke all the fibers rearward as you make each turn. Secure the stem of the feather with a few snug wraps of thread. Clip the stem and finish the fly's head.

Our finished Gray Hackle, Peacock is on the left. Facing it is its brother, a Brown Hackle, Peacock. Either fly can be tied on a down-eye or straight-eye hook. If you want a more realistic—or at least a less obviously fake—caddis pattern, omit the red tail.

TYING A DUBBED WET FLY

This next specimen is more like a proper caddis. While any number of dubbing materials make good bodies on this sort of fly, we'll use a blend of rabbit fur and a synthetic fiber called Antron. A common ingredient in carpet, Antron has optical properties that make it both translucent and reflective. In other words, the stuff sparkles. A blend of fur and Antron has a subtle glitter, and many anglers believe that a wet fly dubbed with such a blend looks like an insect that has tiny gas bubbles under its skin or trapped among the hairs on its body. Some female caddisflies bring a bubble of air with them when they dive into the water to lay their eggs, and an Antron dubbing blend can reproduce this look, too. Of course, it might also be true that glittery flies simply catch the attention of trout.

Fine Antron fibers are packaged and sold as dubbing under a variety of trade names. Umpqua Feather Merchants, for instance, sells this material as Sparkle Blend. It's possible to use 100 percent Antron as dubbing, but the fibers are very slippery (they're plastic, after all) and a little tricky to handle, at least for me. Mixing equal volumes of bunny fur and Antron produces a dubbing that's much easier to use. Blend the rabbit fur first, as you would for the nymphs we tied in chapter 6. Then tease a wad of Antron out of its package. You will probably see that the fibers are much longer than those of the rabbit fur. So, cut the clump of Antron in half, and then blend it with the fur.

Shape the fly's body by wrapping several layers of dubbed thread. When you've finished dubbing the body, make it fuzzy by brushing it with a small, stiff brush. Fuzziness increases the body's apparent bulk and makes it a little more glittery; half of the teased-out fibers are Antron, and all of them can capture tiny air bubbles every time you lift the fly from the water to cast. A toothbrush with the bristles trimmed short makes a good dubbing teaser. A small-bore gun-cleaning brush also works very well for this purpose.

You can tie this type of fly in all the colors of insects. Let's start with a generic pattern that represents any number of tan and brown caddisflies.

Hook: Standard wet fly or 1X-long nymph, sizes 10 through 16.
Thread: Brown or tan.
Body: A blend of natural rabbit and reddish brown Antron dubbing. Brush the body after dubbing it.
Hackle: Brown hen.

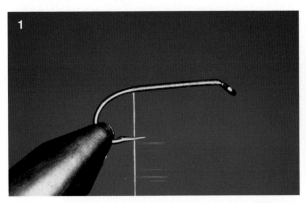

Wrap a base of thread back to the bend of the hook. This is a 1X-long nymph model.

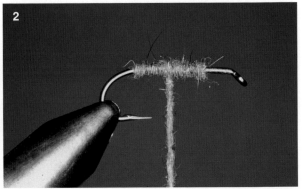

Apply a layer of dubbing to the thread. You can use a slightly thicker layer of material than you did for the nymphs in the last chapter, but twist it just as tightly. Build the body by wrapping several layers.

Make a fairly plump body. Don't crowd the hook eye; you'll need room to wrap the hackle.

Use a small, stiff brush to tease the body and make it fuzzy. Brush the body from front to rear.

Brushing gives the body more apparent bulk and creates a halo effect. If you look closely, you can see the glitter produced by the Antron fibers.

Add a hackle collar—two turns will do—and finish the fly's head.

Among the other color schemes you should try are an olive body with a brown or olive hackle, a gray body with a dun or grizzly hackle, a black body with a black hackle, a cream body with a cream or pale ginger hackle, and a bright green body with a brown or black hackle. In each case, blend approximately equal amounts of fur and Antron to make the dubbing, and use a thread that matches the rest of the dressing. You'll find that these simple wet flies will take trout between hatches and during a caddis emergence, and that they work from early spring until late autumn.

OPTIONS AND VARIATIONS

Add a tail to the simple fly you just tied and you'll have a flymph, a creature that's a cross between a wet fly and a nymph. In effect, it's a soft-hackle mayfly. You can cast a flymph upstream and dead-drift it as you would a nymph pattern, or you can pitch it across the current and swing it as you would a wet fly. The latter method is a good way to catch trout that are feeding on nymphs rising to the surface.

One of my favorite wet flies is a pattern I call a Squirrel Flymph. Like a Gold-Ribbed Hare's Ear nymph, it's not a precise imitation of any one mayfly. But it must suggest many varieties of fish food, because trout, particularly those in streams that have dark bottoms, like it a lot. A Squirrel Flymph is also a killer panfish fly. Here's the recipe.

Squirrel Flymph

Hook: 1X-long nymph, sizes 10 through 14.
Thread: Black.
Tails: Grizzly hen-hackle fibers.
Body: Gray squirrel body fur.
Hackle: Two turns of a grizzly hen-neck feather.

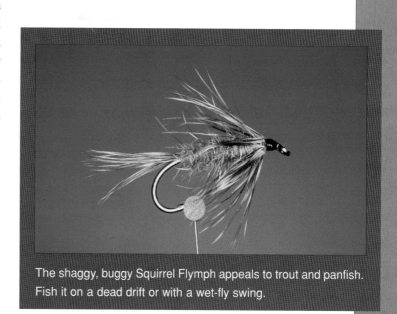

The shaggy, buggy Squirrel Flymph appeals to trout and panfish. Fish it on a dead drift or with a wet-fly swing.

Flymphs make good mayfly emergers. If you want a more detailed pattern, add a wood duck wing like the one on the right-hand fly.

Many fly fishers regard emerger patterns as a fairly recent development. It seems to me, though, that wet flies were the first mayfly emerger patterns. What else does a fly with a tail and a hackle represent as it swings across a stream and rises toward the surface? I suspect that our forebears were more sophisticated anglers than we generally give them credit for being.

A flymph the same size and color as the bug of the day will usually catch trout during the beginning of a hatch. If you want a more detailed lure, add a simple wing made of a small clump of fibers from a flank feather of a wood duck or mallard. This, of course, is essentially the construction of the traditional Cahill and Hendrickson wet flies—tail, dubbed body, hackle, and wing.

Besides tying the patterns you can find in books, make up some flies based on your observations of insects. Here's an example of the sort of thing I mean.

Nameless Wet Fly
Hook: Standard wet fly or 1X-long nymph, size 12 or 14.
Thread: Brown or reddish brown.
Tails: Light brown hen-hackle fibers.
Body: Natural rabbit fur.
Hackle: Two turns of a brown or light brown hen-neck feather.
Wing: A clump of wood duck fibers.

If a stream has mayflies that you might match with a March Brown, Gray Fox, or Light Cahill dry fly, then you can catch trout with this simple, nameless wet fly, particularly during the first stage of a hatch. Vary the colors to make the construction match other mayflies—dun, dark gray, olive, and so forth.

Classic soft-hackle wet flies have bodies made of floss or silk thread, with dubbed thoraxes behind their hackles. They remain superb trout catchers. If you need heavier, quick-sinking wets for fishing in fast or deep water, make the bodies with copper or brass wire instead of silk. Suppliers such

These are essentially classic soft-hackle wets, but with wire bodies instead of the traditional silk. They'll sink quickly and stay deep in fast water.

as Wapsi Fly offer wire in a variety of colors, allowing you to tie imitations of most cad-disflies. Green, orange, and natural copper are all good colors.

Build a wire-bodied wet by attaching a piece of copper wire (plain or colored) at the start of the hook bend. Wrap the wire over about two-thirds of the hook shank, secure it, and cut off the excess. Then dub a thorax with rabbit fur; the dubbed thorax helps the hackle collar keep its shape as the fly swings across the current. Add two wraps of hen hackle and you'll have a bright wet fly with some built-in extra weight.

With their exaggerated hackles, Spider-style wet flies might not seem like good representations of insects. But a Spider's extra-long hackle has loads of action in the water, and fish respond to lures with soft, moving parts. You can turn a soft-hackle wet into a Spider by giving it a partridge or grouse hackle with fibers long enough to reach well beyond the hook bend. Add a tinsel rib if you want. It seems likely that a Spider fished down and across and with an active retrieve can look to a trout like a tiny

When trout have lockjaw, try a Spider-style wet fly. The movement of the extra-long hackle can make stubborn fish decide to eat.

minnow or fry—a very small Soft-Hackle Streamer, as it were. Fished with a traditional wet-fly swing, the same pattern represents a caddis, but one with lively appendages.

All of the constructions in this chapter depend on a folded hackle. Practice that skill and pay attention to the sizes and colors of the insects that you see, and maybe you can write one of next year's articles about the rediscovered wet fly.

Dry flies, or at least flies fished on top of the water, have been around longer than many anglers think. Theodore Gordon didn't invent them. Neither did Frederic Halford. It would take a better historian than I am to determine the earliest uses of floating trout flies, but patterns that we would recognize as dry flies were in use by the 1870s, and probably earlier.

"Patterns that we would recognize as dry flies." As soon as I wrote it, I saw an interesting supposition, or perhaps presumption, in that statement. We 21st-century anglers like to think that we make some pretty sophisticated dry flies—by the crude, simple-minded standards of the past, that is. We flatter ourselves. In the 1870s, a British chap named James Ogden tied exquisite mayfly duns with cut wings every bit as good as any we tie nowadays. Photos of dry flies tied by Theodore Gordon show wings made with a single clump of flank-feather fibers angled back over the body. When you think about it, that sort of wing makes a lot of sense. At rest, real mayfly duns hold their wings together over their backs. Gordon's version of the quill-bodied fly that bears his name is actually a more lifelike dressing than the Quill Gordons we tie nowadays.

Our "classic" dry flies—the Hendrickson, Cahills Light and Dark, the Quill Gordon, the March Brown American, and others—are not the oldest or best dry flies. When we consider the flies of Ogden, Halford, and Gordon, we might classify a pattern such as Roy Steenrod's Hendrickson, with its divided wings made of wood duck fibers, as a third- or fourth-generation dry. It was preceded by a number of other designs, some of them more realistic than a Hendrickson.

So what makes the classics so classic? Why do the Cahills and Hendrickson and related patterns endure? Why have they served as models for so many other patterns, including, at least in method of construction, the famous hair-wing drys tied by Lee Wulff?

Well, they work. The traditional Hendrickson still catches fish during a hatch of *Ephemerella subvaria*. A Wulff pattern bouncing down a riffle still pulls trout up from the bottom.

But there's more to it than utility. The classic dry flies have a special style and elegance. In the vise, in a fly box, or on the water, they're simply nice to look at. My dad has a theory that certain creations—some sloops, Duesenberg and Bugatti automobiles, some side-by-side shotguns, and Marilyn Monroe—simply have perfect lines, forms that we instantly recognize as inherently pleasing. A Light Cahill looks like a trout fly *should*. Even unfortunate people who don't know much about fishing can tell that a Hendrickson or March Brown dry is a trout fly. Besides, we're used to the classic patterns. As a Jungian headshrinker might say, they are part of fly fishing's collective unconscious.

Let's get back to utility. A fly such as a Light Cahill or any of the Wulffs has certain advantages. Its wings, made of a divided clump of fibers, hold up pretty well, do not make the fly spin as the angler casts, and make the pattern land right-side up. No, they're not the most realistic wings a bogus mayfly could have, but they've been good enough to fool millions of trout. When it's tied well and with good hackle, a classic dry has enough buoyancy for most situations. This style of fly, with its upright and divided wings made of hair or fibers from a waterfowl feather, lends itself to no end of tinkering and modifications. The classic patterns are just the beginning.

If you can tie one old-fashioned dry, you can tie many. This Grizzly Riffle Fly, Light Cahill, and Light Hendrickson have essentially the same construction. When tied carefully, they hold up very well. Indeed, if you steam them between outings to remove fish slime, flies like these can easily last through more than a dozen trout.

I prefer this style of wing to most other types. Hackle-tip wings such as those on the standard Adams and Blue-Winged Olive often twist out of alignment or suffer from durability problems. Cut wings (except, notably, those fashioned by James Ogden in the 1870s and described by John Betts in an article for the Autumn/Winter 1996 issue of *Fly Tyer*) tend to create aerodynamic problems and often don't hold up well. Quill-slip wings such as those on the Blue Dun split apart almost instantly. Wings made of clumps of fibers don't have these drawbacks. When you tie a good Light Cahill, you *know* what the thing will do. Clump wings are predictable and reasonably tough. Maybe that's another reason that the classics endure.

Making their upright, divided wings is the main challenge of tying these flies, though it's not the only challenge. The construction method that we shall study produces neat, rugged wings and eliminates the difficulty of making a tidy head. And once you understand the construction, you can use it to make dozens of mayflies in addition to the traditional patterns. You might even find that clump wings replace other styles in your fly boxes, as they have in mine.

But before we construct wings, let's spend a few minutes studying all the components.

THE PARTS

A standard dry-fly hook is made of lighter wire than a nymph or wet-fly hook the same size. Its shank is roughly twice as long as the gap is deep. Dry-fly hooks come with straight, turned-down, and turned-up eyes. A turned-down eye is the traditional style, though a straight eye probably makes more sense these days, since very few anglers use the Turle knot to attach a fly to a tippet. (The Turle knot, incidentally, is among the worst ways to tie a monofilament leader to a hook. If you're still using the Turle, switch to a more modern knot; you'll land more fish.) For the types of flies under discussion here, conventional dry-fly hooks work fine. Every major hook company makes them.

Dry flies require fine thread. Some tiers use extremely skinny thread on drys. That's okay as long as the thread's strength, or lack of it, doesn't become a problem. On all but the tiniest flies, of which I tie very few, I use standard threads such as Danville's Flymaster 6/0, Ultra Thread 70, and size 8/0 Uni-Thread. With reasonably good tying technique, there's no need to use anything finer on a size 14 or 16 dry fly.

The wings of these flies are made of fibers from a duck's flank feather, as on the Light Cahill, or of hair, as on a Wulff pattern or Riffle Fly. A waterfowl flank feather differs from, say, a chicken hackle. The flank feather's fibers are considerably more substantial than those of a chicken feather; they make beautiful, well-defined wings. Mallard and wood duck are the two most common flank feathers used for wing material on dry flies, though other ducks also supply good material. Teal flank, for instance, makes handsome, rugged wings on a variation of the Adams, as we'll see later.

Most hair-wing drys use calf tail or calf body hair, though Lee Wulff used fine buck-tail on the original flies that bear his name. Calf tail's only drawback is that it can be too wavy or crinkled. For making dry-fly wings, look for calf tails that have fairly straight hair. Generally, hair from the base of a tail is straighter and finer than hair from the middle or tip. White is the most commonly used color, but a dyed-gray calf tail furnishes excellent wing material that's closer to the color of a real mayfly dun's wings.

Calf body hair is fine and straight, and it makes lovely wings. It's hard to find in any color but white, though a few catalog houses carry body hair in gray and other colors.

Although household dyes usually don't work very well with fly-tying materials, a strong solution of Rit Pearl Grey dye (color 39) does a good job with calf body hair. Adding several tablespoons of white vinegar to the solution helps the dye to penetrate and bond with the hair.

Stiff, shiny fibers from a rooster hackle are the traditional tail material for dry flies. The stiffness is important, since the tail fibers must support the weight of the fly's aft end on the surface film. These days, many dry-fly capes don't have feathers with fibers long enough for tails on larger dry flies. Breeders have succeeded in producing chickens that have superb hackle feathers, particularly in the smaller sizes, but the birds have relatively few feathers with good tail material. You can,

Vary the density of the tails and hackle to make flies for different types of water. This March Brown has lots of tail fibers and a bushy hackle; it's a good fly for a fast brook. Tied for slower, flatter water, the same pattern would have fewer tails and a sparser hackle.

however, find excellent tail fibers on cheap, imported rooster capes and on capes that have big, broad feathers intended for tying saltwater flies and bass bugs. A package of strung saddle hackles generally has a number of feathers with fibers sufficiently stiff to serve as dry-fly tails.

Patterns with hair wings usually have hair tails, too. Besides calf tail and calf body, a number of other hairs can be used as tails on dry flies. Woodchuck guard hairs make good, exceptionally durable tails. Deer and elk hair also work, as long as the hair doesn't flare very much under thread pressure.

Dry-fly bodies are dubbed with all sorts of natural and synthetic materials. Some traditional patterns call for strange materials. The body of a classic Hendrickson, for instance, is made with pinkish, urine-stained fur from a vixen. Roy Steenrod, the pattern's originator, was a game warden in New York State back in the days when most counties and municipalities had bounties on foxes, and presumably he had no trouble acquiring vixen skins. Relatively few people trap or shoot foxes these days, and even the most slovenly vixen doesn't have a lot of urine-stained fur on her body. Your local fly shop, then, probably doesn't have bins of this material for sale at bargain prices. (If you think that the Hendrickson calls for a strange material, look up the dubbing required for an old British wet fly called the Tup's Indispensable.)

But urine-stained vixen fur doesn't have any magic qualities. Neither do other materials, and the claims of purists notwithstanding, you will not burn in hell for substituting easy-to-get or inexpensive stuff for traditional materials. A Hendrickson is supposed to resemble an *Ephemerella subvaria* mayfly. If it does, trout do not care if the fly's body is made with vixen fur, rabbit, or a synthetic dubbing. As long as the color is right—and you often have considerable leeway here—a great many dubbings will work fine on dry flies.

Natural materials—fur, that is—should be free of guard hairs. This is a good reason for preparing your own dubbings, since most packaged blends contain both underfur and guard hairs. (See chapter 6 for an explanation of how to clean guard hairs from fur.) Fox underfur is very fine and soft, and it makes tight, neat bodies on dry flies. With pieces of gray fox and red fox, you can blend dubbings in several shades of gray and tan. Rabbit underfur also works well and has the advantage of coming in many colors. Muskrat is the traditional material for the Adams and a number of other patterns. Nearly any soft, fine animal fur will make good dry-fly bodies, as long as you remove the guard hairs before blending the stuff.

These days, many tiers use fine-textured synthetic dubbings for dry flies because these materials lend themselves to making slender, smooth, tight bodies. The Super Fine dubbing made by Wapsi Fly (Umpqua Feather Merchants also sells it wholesale) is a superb material for dry flies. Another good one is Ultra Dub by L & L Products. Like fur, these materials can be blended by hand to produce an infinite variety of colors and shades.

I like a dry fly to have a smooth, slender, tightly dubbed body. This has nothing to do with flotation; in fact, a rough or fuzzy body might actually float better because it traps tiny air bubbles. I simply like the looks of a dry fly with a thin, neat body. Besides, real mayflies have smooth bodies.

Traditional dry flies don't float because they're inherently buoyant the way a cork is. They float by sitting atop the surface tension of the water, perched on the tips of their tails and hackles. The hackle, that ruff of stiff fibers produced by wrapping a feather from a rooster's neck around the hook, is the defining feature of a standard dry fly. Without rooster hackles, we wouldn't have such flies as the Light Cahill and Adams.

Good dry-fly hackle has never been sufficiently abundant to be cheap, and these days it's almost shockingly expensive. People who don't fly fish cannot imagine paying $50 or more for part of a dead chicken. I suspect that the price of good hackle discourages many beginners from pursuing this craft, since even a basic assortment of good dry-fly necks—brown, grizzly, cream, and two shades of dun—can set a tier back $250. If I had to start from scratch today, I don't think that I could afford to tie trout flies.

But there's no substitute for good hackle. The feathers from cheap, imported rooster necks sometimes sold as "bargain" or "practice" capes simply won't do the job; they're too short and don't have enough fibers. If you want to tie traditional dry flies, you have to use good hackle.

That doesn't mean that you need to go broke acquiring patches of chicken skin at $50 or $60 a pop. It's possible to economize in several ways. Perhaps you and a friend can split a few rooster necks. If you shop around, you might find dry-fly feathers packaged and sold by the dozen; the cost per feather is relatively high, but your total outlay is much less. Breeders have also developed roosters whose saddle feathers (the long plumes from the bird's lower back) make excellent dry-fly hackles. Dry-fly saddles aren't cheap, but they do yield more flies per dollar than rooster necks do.

You might also decide, as many of us have, to limit your use of traditional, hackled patterns. Many floating flies, such as Foamback Emergers and Spunduns, do not use hackles.

Still, most of us like to have at least a few fly-box compartments filled with old-fashioned drys. Even if you specialize in just a handful of patterns tied the traditional way, you will need top-notch hackle for them. There's no substitute for a good chicken.

TYING TIPS: PROPORTIONS

Most traditional dry flies share a set of more or less standard proportions. These proportions do not necessarily create a perfect replica of the form of a mayfly—none of the classic drys is particularly realistic—but they do produce a lure that lands right-side up and balances nicely on the water. A fly that lands on its face or flops onto its side isn't very useful.

Generally, the wings should be as tall as the hook shank is long. Tails should be as long as the shank; they can be a tad longer. The fly's body should occupy about three-fourths of the hook shank, though the method I use produces a slightly shorter body. The tips of the hackle should not reach the tips of the wings, but they should extend beyond the hook point; three-fourths of the shank length is a good dimension for the hackle fibers. When a dry fly rests on the tips of its tails and hackle, the lowest part of the hook should just touch the surface of the water.

You have a little leeway with those proportions, but not a great deal. Make the tails twice as long as the hook, and the fly will probably tip onto its nose as it falls to the water. If the hackle fibers are much too short, the fly will tip onto its side. Overly bushy, and therefore overly heavy, wings can have the same effect. So, try to stick to the standard proportions.

This Light Cahill hews to traditional proportions. Its wings are a smidgen taller than the hook shank is long, and the hackle fibers are about three-fourths the length of the hook shank. The tiny bit of bare steel behind the hook eye is an old-fashioned touch. Years ago, everyone used the Turle knot to attach dry flies to gut tippets, and that minuscule section of bare hook shank was helpful.

Making the wings is the first step, and for many tiers it's the most difficult. Propping a clump of fibers upright on the hook isn't very hard, and neither is splitting the clump into two smaller bunches. But making neat, even wings that stand up and keep their shape requires some deft work with thread.

BUILDING UPRIGHT, DIVIDED WINGS

I truly cannot remember from whom I learned the method we're about to study. It's certainly not my own invention, though I wish it was. It works with any material and produces handsome, sturdy wings.

To make the photography easier to do and to understand, I used oversize props in the following sequence. Using a big hook and a sizable clump of calf tail or bucktail is also a good way to learn the technique. If you're a novice, don't make yourself crazy trying to build your first pair of wings on a size 14 hook. Clamp a size 4 hook in your vise—any type of hook will do—and work with a clump of stacked hair about 1½ inches long and about ⅛ inch in diameter. As I've noted elsewhere, this sort of practice is not a waste of material; rather, it's an investment that pays off in better flies and less frustration.

If the following process seems complicated, blame it my obsessive personality. I tend to explain things to the point of exhaustion. After you've done it a few times, you can make a pair of upright dry-fly wings in about 10 seconds.

These first few photos show a big clump of calf tail on an immense dry-fly hook. The process is the same on a normal hook. Cut a clump of hair from the tail, clean out the short and broken fibers, and stack the hair to even the tips. Hold the hair on top of the hook with the tips pointing forward. Move the hair until the thread will catch it about one shank length from the tips. Pinch the tuft of hair in place atop the shank and bind it to the hook with 8 or 10 tight wraps of thread. This is much like attaching the wing to a bucktail, but with the hair pointing in the opposite direction.

Trim the butts of the hair at an angle, making a ramp down to the hook shank. You can bind down the butts now or later, after forming the wings. I bound them down now just to show how they should be trimmed to form a slope. After dealing with the wing butts, wind the thread forward to the base of the wing clump.

Pull the hair upright and bring the thread in front of it. While holding the hair up, wrap the tying thread against the base of the wing clump, forming a dam of thread that will prop the hair upright. Don't worry about getting the hair perfectly vertical; close enough is good enough. After propping up the hair, make one turn of thread behind the clump—this is an important step.

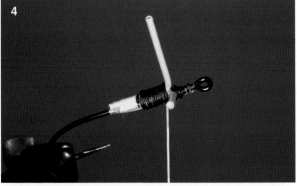

The next step is to divide the hair into two smaller bunches. Simply part it with a needle and spread the two clumps apart. So that you can follow the path of the thread, let's switch to a different prop. The two plastic-coated wires lashed to this size 5/0 hook represent the hair that has been divided into two bunches. White, 20-pound fly-line backing takes the place of tying thread. The wraps of backing already on the hook have been darkened with a marker; the new wraps will stand against the dark background. Note that the backing is hanging behind the wings.

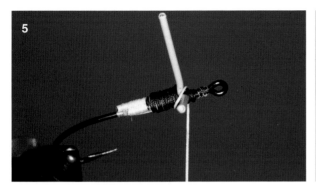

After parting the hair, bring the thread between the wings at an angle from rear to front. Bring the thread down on the far side of the hook.

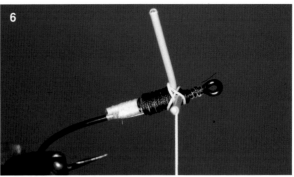

Carry the thread between the wings again, this time going at an angle from front to rear. Make one wrap around the shank behind the wings. At this point, the wings are separated by an X of thread. On a real fly, however, the wings wouldn't be very neat; nor would they be vertical. To make the wings neat and durable, we need to wrap the base of each one.

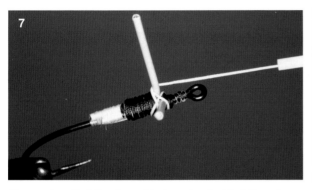

Remember that the thread is hanging behind the wings. Raise the bobbin to the level of the hook shank and begin wrapping the base of the wing on the far side of the hook. Use moderate thread tension. The wraps are made in a clockwise direction when viewed from above.

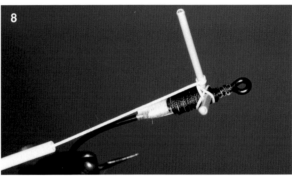

Make several clockwise wraps around the base of the wing. After making each turn of thread, hold the tips of the wing and give the bobbin a gentle tug to tighten the wrap. Generally, a hair wing needs four or five wraps around its base. A wing made of flank-feather fibers probably needs no more than two wraps.

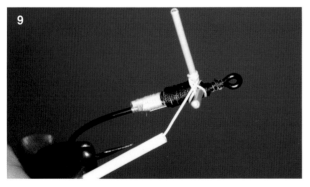

After wrapping the base of the far wing, bring the thread between the wings from front to rear, crossing the hook at an angle. Bring the thread down on the near side of the hook shank. Note that you have reversed the thread's normal direction of travel. In other words, the next turn of thread you make around the hook will be opposite to the direction in which you normally wrap. This, too, is important.

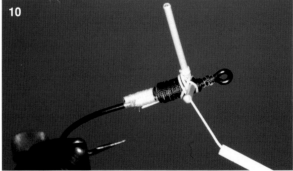

Make one "backward" wrap around the hook shank behind the wings.

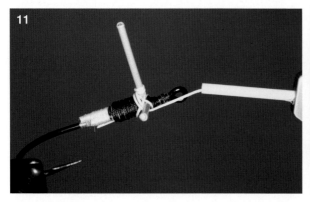

Begin wrapping the wing on the near side of the hook. These wraps form in a counterclockwise direction when viewed from above.

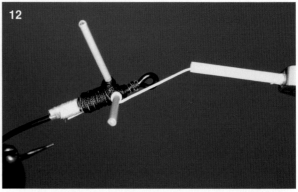

I've darkened all the thread already on the hook so that you can see the new wraps around the base of the near wing. Remember that these wraps go counterclockwise. Using moderate thread tension, make as many wraps as you did on the other wing. Hold the tips of the wing while you tighten each wrap.

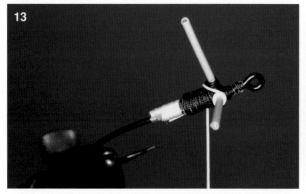

After wrapping the base of the wing, bring the thread between the wings from front to rear. It crosses the hook at an angle and goes down on the far side of the shank. You have now returned the thread to its normal direction of travel.

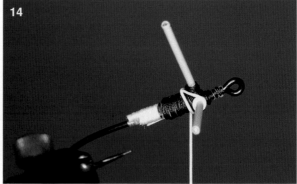

Make one wrap behind the wings. You're done. If necessary, you can tug and pinch the wings into better alignment.

Here's the hair shown in the first three photos. See how the base of each wing has been wrapped? It's generally a good idea to add a tiny drop of cement to the wraps on hair wings. With flank-feather wings, do not use cement; it will wick up the fibers and glue them together.

Yes, it seems like a lot of unnecessary fussing with thread. But it's really not. This process makes the neatest, sturdiest wings possible. The first X of thread pushes the two clumps apart. The wraps around the base of each clump squeeze the fibers into a tidy bundle. You finish wrapping each wing by bringing the thread between the wings from front to rear, which helps pull the clump upright.

This method works with hair and flank-feather fibers. Hair, of course, should be cleaned and then aligned in a small hair stacker before it is attached to the hook. Think for a moment before tilting the hair stacker on its side and separating the halves. Make sure that the tips of the hair will be pointing in the right direction (toward the hook eye) before you remove the clump from the stacker. If you have to pass the hair from hand to hand and turn the clump around to get it pointing the right way, you will almost certainly unstack it. After tapping the hair stacker on your desk, tilt it toward the rear of the hook and then separate the halves.

The tips of flank-feather wings should also be aligned. On a large feather, the fibers on the tip section are already fairly even, so you can cut the tips out of two feathers and use them to make a pair of wings. Since I'm a cheapskate who hates to waste any usable material, I'll painstakingly preen the fibers on the midsection of a flank feather until their tips are aligned, and then cut the bunch from the stem. By combining two or three such bunches, I end up with enough material for a pair of wings. Less stingy tiers might not want to go to the trouble. The fluffy stuff on the bottom of a flank feather has no use, and should be stripped off and discarded before you tackle the useful fibers.

Hair wings usually require more wraps around their bases than flank-feather wings do. Make four or five wraps for each hair wing, two wraps for each wing made of mallard or wood duck fibers. Apply a tiny drop of cement to the thread at the bases of hair wings; do not cement mallard or wood duck wings.

Trim the wing butts at an angle to form a ramp down to the hook shank. When you trim the tail butts, which is more easily done before attaching the fibers to the hook, try to gauge their length so that they blend into the ramp created by the butts of the wing fibers. The point is to make a smooth, even foundation for the body.

You will see below that I take a somewhat unusual approach to attaching the hackle and dubbing the body. After making the wings and tying on the tails, I attach the stripped butt of the hackle feather behind the wings, tying it athwart the hook with an X-wrap or crisscross wrap and then binding the butt to the hook shank. When I'm done, the feather is sticking out of the fly behind the wings, more or less at a right angle to the hook. Then I dub a full body. That is, I dub up the point where the hackle feather is attached, and then gently pull the feather to the rear and make a couple of wraps of dubbing behind the wings and in front of them, giving the fly a dubbed thorax. Then I wrap the hackle over the dubbed thorax.

This method has several benefits. It secures the butt of the feather very well. It gives the stem of the hackle feather a relatively soft surface to sink into, which helps all the fibers stand upright. The dubbed thorax also acts as a tiny cushion when a fish chews on the fly, lessening the likelihood that a trout's teeth will cut the hackle stem. Since the butt end of the hackle is attached in the fly's body area, the only operation I have to perform at the front end of the hook is tying down the hackle tip after wrapping the feather; this virtually guarantees making a small, neat head. And the dubbed thorax also gives me some leeway in the size of the hackle feather; if I have an otherwise good feather that's a tad too small, I can make the fly's thorax a mite fatter to make up the difference.

How much hackle to use—that is, how many wraps to make—depends to some extent on the purpose of the fly. Flies for fast, rough water generally have full, dense hackles made with eight or more wraps. But while a dense hackle can help flotation a little, it also obscures a fly's body and wings. In general, sparse hackles are better, particularly on flies for moderate or slow water. On a size 12 or 14 Light Cahill, for instance, five turns of hackle will do.

TYING A MODERN CLASSIC: THE GRIZZLY RIFFLE FLY

This Wulff-style, hair-wing fly was invented in the 1970s by a gentleman named Dick Surrette, the founder and first editor of *Fly Tyer* magazine. I learned about it from *The Book of Fly Patterns,* by Eric Leiser, in the 1980s. The Grizzly Riffle Fly uses common materials of which I had plenty, so I tied a bunch and caught loads of trout with them. It quickly became one of my favorite dry flies. In 1993, I became the editor of *American Angler,* the magazine that *Fly Tyer* had by then turned into. In 1995, Abenaki Publishers, my employer, relaunched *Fly Tyer,* and for five years I was its editor. So, the Grizzly Riffle Fly was created by a man who founded a unique magazine that I helped to revive.

It's a good fly, useful not only as an attractor pattern in fast water (as its name implies), but also as a high-visibility fly during evening hatches and spinner falls. In sizes 10 and 8, it's a fine dry fly for smallmouth bass. I don't doubt that, tied on the right hooks and with plenty of hackle, it would catch salmon and steelhead.

Those are personal reasons for selecting the Grizzly Riffle Fly for this exercise. The practical reason is that tying it will teach you everything you need to know about constructing old-fashioned drys. Once you can tie this fly, you can easily make patterns such as the Light Cahill and Hendrickson; the only difference is that wings made of flank-feather fibers require fewer wraps of thread around their bases.

Here are the materials you'll need.

Hook: Standard dry fly, sizes 10 through 16.
Thread: Black.
Wings: Calf tail or calf body hair.
Tails: Originally, white calf tail. I often substitute woodchuck guard hairs, and that's what the fly below has. Gray calf tail also makes nice tails on this fly.
Hackle: Grizzly, from either a rooster neck or a dry-fly saddle patch. As a rule, flies like this have full, bushy hackle collars.
Body: Originally, muskrat fur. In the past, I often tied Grizzly Riffle Flies with Ultra Dub material in a color called "warm gray." These days, I use gray Super Fine dubbing.

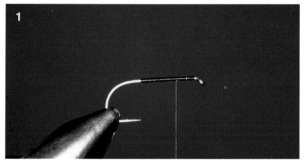

Attach the thread behind the hook eye and wrap a base on most of the shank. Return the thread to a spot one-fourth to one-third of the way back from the eye. Try not to attach dry-fly wings too close to the hook eye; if you don't leave enough room, you'll have trouble with the hackle and head.

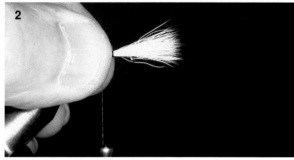

Clean and stack a clump of calf tail or, as shown here, body hair. Remember that this clump will become two wings; use enough hair. Hold the hair over the hook with the tips forward. The tie-in spot is roughly one shank length from the tips. Pinch the hair and hook shank, make sure that your fingertips are even with the tying thread, and begin binding the hair to the hook. This is similar to tying the wing on a bucktail, but backward—the hair points forward and the wraps of thread progress toward the rear of the hook.

Make as many tight wraps of thread as you can without going past the midpoint of the shank. On a relatively large hook like this one (it's a size 10, chosen to make the photography less difficult), you can easily make a dozen wraps. On a size 14 hook, you might have room for only eight turns of thread. In any case, leave room to trim the wing butts and tie in the tails.

Trim the wing butts at an angle or stagger-cut them to make a ramp down to the hook shank. Don't bind down the butts yet. Advance the thread to the base of the wing clump.

Pull the hair upright and bring the thread in front of it. While holding the hair upright, wrap against the front of the clump, forming a band or dam of thread that will prop up the hair. Don't worry if the hair isn't perfectly vertical when you let go of it.

Bring the thread behind the hair. Divide the clump of hair into two bunches and pull them apart. As described above, in the first sequence, make an X-wrap to separate the wings.

Wrap the bases of the wings according to the instructions in the first photo sequence. Hair wings generally need four or five wraps around each base. Push, tug, or pinch the wings into their final alignment. Apply a tiny drop of cement to the wraps.

Bind down the wing butts, forming a smooth ramp of thread down to the hook shank. Wrap the thread back to the start of the bend.

Body and Hackle

Tie in the tails (woodchuck guard hairs on this example). It helps to trim the butts to length before attaching the material to the hook. Note how the butts of these tails just overlap the ramp created by the wing butts.

Finish binding down the butts of the tail fibers. Note that the underbody is fairly smooth. Advance the thread to a spot slightly behind the wings. Select a hackle feather with fibers about three-fourths the length of the hook shank. Cut off the fluffy section of the feather and discard it. Strip a few fibers from the butt end of the hackle, making a little handle.

This example is a fairly large dry fly, so it will get two hackles. On a smaller fly, one good hackle feather suffices. Tie the stripped butt(s) of the feather(s) across the hook shank with an X-wrap of thread. This X-wrap is exactly like that used to separate the wings (see steps 5 and 6 in the first sequence), only smaller. At this point, the feathers are sticking out of the side of the fly.

Bind the butt(s) of the feather(s) against the side of the hook shank. The feathers remain roughly perpendicular to the hook, which simplifies making a neat first wrap of hackle. Furthermore, this method locks the feathers to the hook so that they can't pull out when you start to wrap them.

Twist a thin layer of dubbing onto the thread and begin dubbing the body. This is Super Fine dubbing; note how thinly it can be applied. Simply ignore the hackle feathers as you dub the fly's body; let your hand brush them out of the way as you make each wrap of dubbed thread.

When you reach the hackle feathers, gently pull them rearward and make a couple of wraps of dubbed thread between the feathers and the rear of the wings. Then make a couple of wraps of dubbing in front of the wings. This dubbed thorax is not a traditional feature on this type of fly, but it helps support the bases of the wings and provides a good foundation for the hackle. Just be sure to leave room for the head—better to leave a little too much than too little.

Grab the tip of the feather (or the tip of one of them, on a fly with two hackles) with your hackle pliers. Wind the feather forward over the thorax. On a normal trout fly—a size 12 to 16, say—make two or three wraps of hackle behind the wings and another two or three in front of them. This big, bushy fly gets four wraps on each side of the wings with each feather. When you reach the head area, hold the hackle at an angle as shown and secure it with two wraps of thread.

Wind and secure the second hackle as you did the first. Make another few wraps of thread to lock the feathers to the hook. I generally clip off both of the excess hackle tips at the same time; some tiers clip the first hackle before wrapping the second one.

Clip the excess hackle tips. Finish the fly's head; try to keep it small and neat. After whip-finishing the thread, give the head at least one coat of good cement. For a novice, all of this goes more easily (or with less difficulty, depending on your frame of mind) on a size 10 or 12 hook than on a 14 or 16. So, if this type of fly is new to you, tie a dozen big specimens before trying some on smaller hooks. With a little practice, you'll have no trouble making old-fashioned dry flies on hooks as least as small as size 16.

The wings of this Adams are made of teal-flank fibers rather than the usual hackle tips. They hold up better than the standard wings, and fish like them just fine.

After a little practice, you will be able to tie rugged hair and flank-feather wings on smaller flies. The fly immediately behind the Hendrickson in the center is a Hair-Wing Sulfur. The fly on the far left and the two on the right are various imitations of blue-winged olive mayflies.

OPTIONS AND VARIATIONS

The techniques we've studied will let you build a bunch of classic dry flies found in pattern books: the Cahills, Hendrickson, Gray Fox, March Brown, most Wulffs, and others. But those are just the beginning.

The Blue Dun is a fine old pattern that resembles several early-season mayflies, but its quill-slip wings are troublesome to make and fragile in the field. So, replace them with wings made of mallard-flank fibers or gray calf tail, saving the pattern's dun hackle-fiber tails, muskrat-fur body, and dun hackle. You can do the same with other old patterns, such as George LaBranche's Whirling Dun, one of the great dry flies of the early 20th century.

A number of standard dry flies have wings made of hackle tips. Though less delicate and difficult than quill slips, hackle-tip wings also have problems. They tend to twist to one side as you mount them, and they're easily bent out of shape. Replace them with clump wings. The grizzly hackle tips used on the Adams, for instance, can be replaced with teal-flank fibers. Dick Talleur has written about this pattern, which he calls a Teal-Wing Adams and which catches fish every bit as well as the standard version does. Here's a recipe.

Teal-Wing Adams

Hook: Standard dry fly, sizes 12 through 20.
Thread: Black.
Wings: Well-marked fibers from a teal flank feather.
Tails: Mixed brown and grizzly hackle fibers. A small clump of woodchuck guard hairs is a sturdy, buoyant substitute.
Body: Muskrat fur or dark gray synthetic dubbing.
Hackle: Brown and grizzly.

Other patterns can have their hackle-tip wings replaced with flank-feather fibers or hair. Trout are perfectly happy with an otherwise standard Sulfur that has wings made of mallard flank or gray calf body hair. Nothing else on the pattern changes. If you can manage clump wings on a size 18 hook, you can use the same trick on Blue-Winged Olive and Pale Morning Dun flies. On a frame this small, mallard flank is easier to handle than calf hair, though an experienced tier can tie hair wings on a size 18 hook.

Clump wings work fine on big, long patterns that represent drakes or *Hexagenia* mayflies. For these jumbo drys, use long-shank, light-wire hooks such as the Mustad 94831 or Daiichi 1280 in sizes 8 and 10 (and perhaps size 6 for a Hex pattern). If you want to save a few bucks on hooks, you can tie big mayflies on inexpensive Aberdeen models such as the Mustad 3261. Moose mane or hair from the brown portion of a bucktail is a good tail material for drake patterns. Since they have long bodies, these flies have room for a rib, which adds segmentation and reinforces the body. The general construction method, however, is just like that of a Grizzly Riffle Fly. Here's a flexible parts list for Brown Drakes and Green Drakes.

Except for their longer hooks, these drake patterns are built just like smaller, standard flies. A longer body provides room for a rib, as on the fly on the right. The tails of both flies are bucktail.

Look at insects, trust your eyes, and don't be afraid to experiment. The fly on the left is a more or less standard Light Hendrickson. In the middle is a darker Hendrickson with hair tails and wings; it's a good fast-water fly. The version on the right has standard hackle-fiber tails, but its durable wings are made of highly visible, light gray calf tail.

Drakes

Hook: Long-shank dry fly, size 8 or 10.
Thread: Brown on a Brown Drake, or greenish olive on a Green Drake.
Wings: Wood duck flank or gray calf tail. Fish don't seem to care; the hair wing is more visible in evening light.
Tails: Brown bucktail or hair from the brown portion of a dyed-yellow tail.
Body: Tan dubbing on a Brown Drake, or greenish olive dubbing on a Green Drake.
Rib (optional): Heavy, dark brown thread. I use a permanent marker to stain a piece a Kevlar thread, which makes a very tough rib. Tie off the rib behind the wings, before dubbing the fly's thorax.
Hackle: Brown or grizzly and brown. Use a few more turns of hackle than you would on a standard dry fly.

Trust your eyes and don't be afraid to replace materials on standard patterns. When I look at the wings of a Hendrickson mayfly, for instance, I don't always see a color best duplicated by a flank feather from a wood duck. Sometimes, I see smoky gray wings. So, I've tried Hair-Wing Hendricksons tied with gray calf tail, and the trout have approved.

Unnaturally bright or colorful wings make a fly easier to see on rough water or in poor light. A Riffle Fly winged with fluorescent yellow calf tail looks strange in daylight, but it doesn't disappear as it bounces down a riffle in the gloaming. Phil Monahan, the editor of *American Angler,* has caught a lot of trout with a goofy little dry fly that has hot-pink wings. In the dim light under the canopy that shades a mountain brook, Phil's pink-winged fly is as visible as a red-and-white bobber.

OLD-FASHIONED DRYS

Of course, you might not want to be seen casting a fly with hot-pink wings on a famous trout stream frequented by serious, Latin-mumbling hatch-matchers. But if you do, you might as well cast a fly that has sturdy, well-made pink wings. And who knows—maybe the fly will be a classic a century from now.

Parachute flies fascinate many anglers. Maybe fly fishers love the idea of a horizontal hackle that slows the fly's descent, or perhaps they like a fly that sits low in the water, its body awash in the surface film. I suspect that some of the fascination derives from the perceived difficulty of tying parachutes. A lot of tiers struggle with these flies, and more than a few give up on them.

Parachute flies present two main challenges: creating a solid base around which to wrap the horizontal hackle, and securing the hackle after it has been wrapped. On a conventionally hackled fly, a tier wraps the feather around the hook shank; on a parachute, he has to wrap it around the base of the wing, which is less rigid than a steel fishhook. The tying-off problem arises from the orientation of the hackle. A tier needs somehow to catch the feather's stem with the thread and bind it to the hook, but he has to avoid trapping a bunch of hackle fibers in the process.

Both problems are easily solved. Of course, both are easily avoided, too. A parachute pattern accomplishes little that can't be achieved by other means. Trimming the hackle of a conventional dry fly will bring the body closer to the water and give the bug a bigger footprint. Whether a horizontal hackle does indeed function as a parachute has always struck me as a moot question. *Any* hackled dry fly falls to the water gently—more softly, in many cases, than real insects do.

Still, parachutes are elegant and effective flies, and most fly tiers want to make them. Solving one of the tying challenges begins with a look at materials.

A horizontal hackle makes a wide footprint on the surface film (like the outspread legs of a mayfly) and brings the fly's body close to the water (again, like that of a real mayfly). A couple of simple tricks solve the challenge of making this type of hackle.

THE PARTS

You can tie parachutes with the same hooks, threads, tail materials, and dubbings that you use for other dry flies. Stiff, shiny hackle fibers are the original tail material, but some tiers have switched to synthetic fibers such as Microfibbetts or Betts Tailing Fibers. Although all sorts of dubbings work on parachute flies, synthetic materials such as Wapsi's Super Fine Dubbing make a lot of sense on a fly that floats with its body awash. If you use natural fur, apply a little floatant or waterproofing agent to the body before using the fly.

Use polypropylene yarn for the wing post. Poly yarn does not necessarily make a better post than calf tail or other natural hairs, but it can simplify tying a parachute. Because the fibers of poly yarn are not tapered like those of natural materials, you can attach a long piece of it to the hook. A long piece of poly

Polypropylene yarn is the easiest material with which to make the wing post on a parachute fly. This Light Cahill Parachute has a few extra tail fibers and an extra turn of hackle, making it a good choice in choppy water.

yarn is easier to handle than a short clump of hair. After tying the fly, cut the poly-yarn post to length.

Poly yarn has another construction advantage. You can attach it across the hook shank with a couple of X-wraps of thread, much as you would make the wings of some spinner patterns. After tying the piece of yarn athwart the hook, lift both ends upright so that the fibers become a single clump. Then wrap the tying thread around the base of the post to create a firm foundation on which to wrap the hackle. This method adds no bulk to the hook shank. In contrast, a clump of hair has to be bound *along* the hook shank and then elevated, a process that creates a sizable lump on the hook. That lump complicates both making the fly's body and wrapping its horizontal hackle.

White seems the most common color for parachute posts, but poly yarn comes in lots of colors. Gray and tan look more like the wings of real mayflies. Yellow, chartreuse, and orange poly yarn make posts that are easy to see in poor light.

Use a hackle feather with fibers that are at least as long as the hook shank. The wide, circular footprint of a parachute fly means that you don't need to use top-quality dry-fly hackle. A parachute will float fine with four or five wraps of a Grade 3 feather or even a hackle from an imported rooster neck. With good hackle, it's often possible to tie two flies with each feather. Either way, you save a little dough. When they're made with poly-yarn posts and inexpensive hackle, parachutes are relatively cheap to produce.

TYING TIPS

The stiffer the base of the wing post, the easier it is to wrap the hackle. Years ago, a few companies made special parachute hooks that had vertical posts; Partridge revived the idea in the 1990s. But wrapping the base of the poly-yarn post and then cementing the wraps will make a foundation that's more than sufficiently rigid.

The most important parachute-fly secret is very simple: Whip-finish the thread *before* wrapping the hackle. Don't cut the thread; just make a three- or four-turn whip finish to knot it to the hook. As you will see in a minute, this trick greatly simplifies securing the hackle feather. I wish I remembered where I learned this method, because it's a wonderful trick and I'd like to give credit to its originator.

Let's do it once so that you can see how it works.

SECURING A HORIZONTAL HACKLE

The following sequence deals only with winding and securing a parachute hackle; it doesn't show a complete fly. As I have elsewhere in this book, I used an oversize hook and jumbo materials to simplify the photography. If you've never tied parachutes, you might want to practice with similarly large components until you get the hang of the technique.

The base of the wing post has been wrapped with thread and cemented to make a rigid foundation. When you attach the hackle feather, tie it in so that it's pointing toward the rear on the far side of the hook, as this one is. Then whip-finish the thread right in front of the wing post.

Here's what the whip finish accomplishes. With the thread knotted to the hook, you can raise the bobbin in front of the hook until the thread is horizontal. You can work the thread in between the fibers of a horizontal parachute hackle without trapping any of them. This whip-finish knot takes the trouble out of tying this type of fly.

Grab the tip of the hackle with your pliers. Wrap the hackle around the post in a counterclockwise direction as viewed from above. Make each wrap *under* the preceding one; that is, keep the stem of the feather under the fibers of the collar. Four or five wraps will suffice.

After making the final wrap of hackle, let the hackle pliers hang off the far side of the hook, as shown here. Large, English-style pliers are more than heavy enough to keep the hackle taut.

Lift the bobbin in front of the hook until the thread is even with the shank. If you had not whip-finished the thread, this step would be impossible. Guide the thread between the hackle fibers.

Bring the thread down on the far side of the hook, trapping the stem of the feather against the hook. Keep the thread taut as you bring the bobbin under the hook. You now have one wrap of thread securing the hackle tip to the hook shank—and, for now, that's enough.

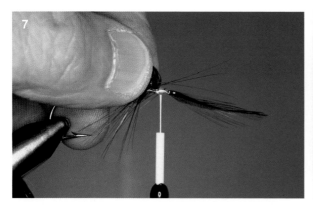

Keep the thread tight while you carefully stroke and pull the front half of the hackle collar out of the way. Let the bobbin hang while you remove the pliers from the tip of the feather. Make another few wraps of thread around the hackle stem and hook shank. Then clip the hackle tip and whip-finish the thread.

Pulling half of the fibers out of the way will have made a mess of the collar. No problem—pull the wing upright and push the hackle fibers back into position. If one or two fibers stick out at a crazy angle, clip them with your fine scissors.

Once you master this technique, you'll find parachutes no more difficult than other flies. Indeed, you will probably be able to knock them out more quickly than conventional dry flies.

TYING A QUILL GORDON PARACHUTE

Theodore Gordon did not invent dry flies. He was almost certainly not the first American to use them. But Gordon did much to popularize floating flies in the United States, and he is generally regarded as the father of American dry-fly fishing.

The fly we call the Quill Gordon (or Gordon Quill) bears only a rough resemblance to the quill-bodied pattern dressed by Gordon himself. The original version used the same materials as the contemporary fly—dun tails and hackle, wood duck wing, and stripped-peacock body—but Gordon tied his flies on longer hooks than those we use today, and he made the wing (note the singular noun) with a clump of wood duck fibers slanted back over the body. With its single, rearward-leaning wing and relatively long abdomen, the original Quill Gordon does an excellent job of representing the form of a mayfly dun. Indeed, its shape is better than those of most modern dry flies.

Although it has changed a bit over the decades, Gordon's best-known fly remains a favorite early-season pattern, particularly among eastern anglers. Generally fished as an imitation of the iron fraudator mayfly, *Epeorus pleuralis*, the Quill Gordon can represent several species of medium-to-dark mayflies. It's also a good searching pattern. Trout just seem to like this fly.

Our parachute version replaces the traditional, fragile, and troublesome stripped-peacock-quill body with dubbing. That's heresy in the minds of some anglers, but it's a practical substitution. No, the effect is not exactly the same—dubbing cannot replicate the beautiful, light-and-dark segmentation of stripped peacock—but the right dubbing blend can come very close to the overall color of a stripped quill. Fine-fibered synthetic materials such as Super Fine and Ultra Dub work very well for this job. Mix gray, tan, and brown material until you have a blend the same color as stripped peacock. A few stripped quills wrapped around hooks will give you a basis for comparison. Start with two parts of gray, two parts of tan, and one part of brown, and then tinker with the mix until you like its looks. I like to add just a little olive material to the blend.

The other substitution we will make is the wing material. A tuft of wood duck fibers can be fashioned into a parachute post, but poly yarn is easier to work with. Tan poly yarn might seem close to the color of the original wing material, but gray polypropylene more accurately matches the color of the real insect's wings.

Here's the parts list for our Quill Gordon Parachute.

Hook: Standard dry fly, size 12 or 14.
Thread: Gray 6/0 or 8/0.
Tails: Medium or dark dun hackle fibers.
Wing post: Gray or tan poly yarn.
Body: Grayish tan dubbing, as described above.
Hackle: Medium dun.

We'll use an optional trick on this fly. A real mayfly's tails are separated, and we'll try to reproduce that look by splitting our fly's tail clump with a piece of thread. This is only one way to divide the tails of a dry fly. The Spunduns in chapter 11 show another method, and fly tiers have devised many more. I learned the thread-between-the-tails trick from one of the "Tying Tips" published in *American Angler* or *Fly Tyer* (or maybe *American Angler & Fly Tyer*) many years ago, before I was involved with the magazines. It pays to have a good memory for arcane things.

Tails and Post

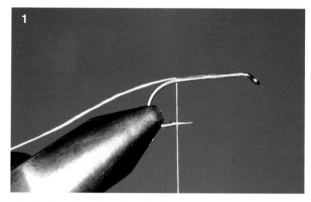

Attach the thread to the hook, but don't cut off the tag end. Instead, keep wrapping over the tag end until you reach the rear of the shank, so that you have a long piece of thread hanging off the aft end of the hook. You can also tie on a separate piece of heavier thread, as I did here.

Tie on a clump of tail fibers. Wrap the tying thread to a spot even with the point of the hook. Lift the thread hanging off the rear of the hook up and through the middle of the tail clump. Bring this thread forward and bind it to the hook with two wraps of tying thread.

Pull on the end of the tail-splitting thread to tighten it. As you do, the thread will divide the tail fibers into two clumps. Bind down the tail-splitting thread and cut off the excess. This method will sometimes cause a couple of tail fibers to stick up at wild angles. That's why you have scissors—simply snip them off.

Cut a piece of poly yarn about 2 inches long. Use a needle to split the yarn into three or four strands; you don't need much material to make the wing post. Attach one of the thin strands of poly yarn across the hook with two crisscross wraps of tying thread.

Body and Horizontal Hackle

Pull the ends of the poly yarn up. Wrap the base of the post with tying thread. Make more than just a few wraps—wind the thread up the post and back down to cover enough of the base to create an adequate foundation for the hackle. Carefully apply a droplet of flexible cement to the wraps to stiffen the base of the post. Note that this method of making a post adds no bulk whatsoever to the hook shank.

Dub the body, keeping it thin and sleek. Make one wrap of dubbed thread in front of the wing post. Attach the hackle feather so that it points rearward on the far side of the hook shank. After tying on the feather, whip-finish the thread. That last step is important—don't forget to knot the thread to the hook.

Wrap the hackle around the base of the post, winding it counterclockwise when viewed from above. Make each wrap under the previous one. After making four or five wraps, let your hackle pliers hang off the far side of the hook.

Thanks to the whip finish, you can bring the thread up in front of the fly and sneak it between the hackle fibers. Then bring the bobbin down on the far side of the hook, trapping the hackle stem with one wrap of the thread.

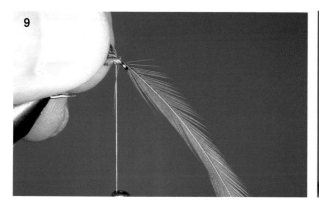

9

10

Gently pull the hackle fibers out of the way. Make another few wraps of thread around the hackle tip, securing it to the hook. Remove your pliers and clip the excess hackle. While holding the fibers out of the way, whip-finish the thread.

Pull the wing upright and press any errant hackle fibers back into alignment. Trim the wing to length; it should be about as long as the hook shank. To make an extra-sturdy parachute, apply a tiny droplet of flexible cement to the topmost wrap of hackle stem; I generally don't bother with this. Use a fine applicator to apply cement to the fly's head.

OPTIONS AND VARIATIONS

You can tie practically any standard dry fly as a parachute. Simply replace the divided wings with a post of white, gray, or tan poly yarn, and wrap the hackle horizontally. Use the same body, tail, and hackle colors that you'd use on the conventional version of the fly.

Tied sparsely, parachutes are excellent slow-water flies. Made with lots of tails and an extra turn of hackle, a parachute has good buoyancy on rough water. Tie them both ways.

Some dry flies have two hackles. The Adams and March Brown American, for instance, both have collars made with two feathers. When I tie a parachute version of such a fly, I generally use only one hackle.

Parachutes tied with white or pale gray hackles are good spent-spinner patterns. Even though it's trimmed short, the white post makes this type of fly easier to see on the water than other spinner patterns. Trimming a few of hackle fibers provides easier access to the hook eye.

On a Parachute Adams, I'll replace the traditional mixed hackle with a dyed-brown grizzly feather or a barred variant feather that has a tannish background with dark bars. It's possible to use two feathers on a parachute by wrapping both at once, but it's not easy. I'd rather wrap a single feather that approximates the look of the standard hackle. Trout don't seem to mind.

Poly yarn can be spotted or mottled with a black permanent marker so that it looks like the grizzly wings of an Adams or the real wings of a *Callibaetis* mayfly. Mark the yarn before tying it to the hook.

Sparsely tied flies such as the Pale Evening Dun Parachute on the right work very well on slow, flat water. On fast, rough water, use a parachute with more tails and a denser hackle like those of the Light Cahill on the left. To simplify attaching it to the tippet, the front of the smaller fly's hackle has been trimmed.

Although they're rarely tied for the purpose, parachutes make pretty good spinner flies. To represent the glassy wings of a spent mayfly, use a white or pale gray hackle. Make the wing post with white poly yarn, and trim it short (about half of the shank length) after securing the hackle. The short, upright post makes a parachute spinner easy to see on the water.

Some of a parachute fly's hackle fibers can get in the way when you tie the fly to your tippet. A few of them might even become caught in the knot. If you find this annoying, snip the fibers that point over the eye of the hook, making a narrow V in the front of the hackle.

Remember always to whip-finish the thread before wrapping the hackle, and you will have no problems with these elegant, deadly flies. Even when they become easy to tie, parachutes remain fascinating—particularly to the trout.

"Can you show me how to tie an Irresistible?" asked the big guy who had taken the seat next to me the first night of fly-tying class.

"Well, sure," I said. "I can show you. But that's a fairly tricky fly. It's better to begin with—"

"Tonight?" he asked.

"Well, actually, I was planning to begin the course with—"

"I really like Irresistibles," the man said. "I don't care about bucktails and I hardly ever fish nymphs. I wanna tie Irresistibles. Can you show me how? That's why I signed up for this."

"Yes, I can *show* you. But not tonight. And it won't do you much good just to watch me tie one. They're hard. You need to learn a few things before tackling—"

"I wanna tie Irresistibles," he said. "You just show me and I'll figure it out."

We compromised: After the class's third meeting, he stayed and watched me tie an Irresistible. He stayed after the fourth class, too, and watched me tie another one. He didn't figure it out, probably because he hadn't paid much attention to learning any of the basic fly-tying skills. There *had* to be some trick, he insisted, implying that I was holding back a vital secret, even though he'd watched me build two Irresistibles in front of him. He didn't come to the last two classes. I've sometimes wondered if he ever figured it out.

Like many other things, including fishing, fly tying is cumulative. While this craft might not involve learning a perfectly linear progression of skills, it does require that one acquire certain bits of knowledge and develop certain types of dexterity before moving to the next level. My impatient student wouldn't accept that proposition. *Show me the trick,* he demanded (as if Joe Messinger's Irresistible requires only one), *and let me get outta here.* Such persons rarely become fly tiers. Or good fishermen, for that matter.

The two caddisfly constructions in this chapter are neither complex nor difficult, but they still require an accumulation of skills. Al Troth's wonderful Elk Hair Caddis, the model for dozens of other hair-wing caddisflies, is about as standard a pattern as one can find. It can be tied in no end of sizes and colors, and it works on all types of water. Nearly every trout fisherman has Elk Hair Caddis or one of the

Most caddisfly species can be represented by various versions of the Elk Hair Caddis. Making neat, sturdy wings is the main challenge in tying these flies; the skills used on bucktails apply to hair-wing caddis patterns.

Trimming the underside of a caddis's hackle makes the fly less likely to tip over. It also gives the fly a more realistic posture on the water.

What they lack in elegance, Fathead Caddis make up for in utility. These simple, no-hackle flies float with their bodies awash. Trout love them.

design's many progeny in his fly boxes; every list of 12 essential flies contains Al Troth's best-known creation.

The Elk Hair Caddis and similar flies seem simple, but tying them well requires mastery of a few basic skills: dubbing a body, palmering a hackle and counterwinding it with wire, and attaching a clump of hair squarely and securely atop a hook. For most people, making a neat, sturdy wing is the most difficult part of tying this fly. The world is full of caddis patterns with cock-eyed, off-center wings that fall apart after a dozen casts. If you want to tie good caddisflies, learn to tie *very* good bucktails; practice the stuff in chapter 4.

The other variety of caddis that we shall examine also calls for skills best learned on larger flies. A Fathead Caddis borrows the deer-hair head of a Muddler Minnow. I've included it not only because it catches fish and floats well, but also because a Fathead Caddis is a no-hackle pattern, and therefore inexpensive to make. Anyone can learn to spin a clump of hair, but a size 14 dry-fly hook is probably not the place to do it. Tying the Marabou Muddlers in chapter 5 is a better way to learn how to work with deer hair. If you've never spun a clump of hair, tie a dozen Muddlers before trying it on smaller hooks.

These two are not the only good caddis designs, and they're not always the best imitations of caddisflies. On flat, slow water, for instance, a more realistic pattern with feather wings will often outfish a hair-wing fly. But in most situations, one (and sometimes either) of these two constructions will catch trout. Tied well, both are very durable flies. And neither calls for unusual materials.

THE PARTS

Any of the standard dry-fly hooks will work as the chassis of an Elk Hair or Fathead Caddis. The Elk Hair Caddis's wing makes a down-eye hook the best choice; Fathead Caddis can be tied on hooks with turned-down or straight eyes.

Both flies have dubbed bodies. Nearly any material will work. Hare's-mask dubbing is the original material for the Elk Hair Caddis, but rabbit fur cut from Zonker strips will make an equally good body. For bushy dry flies like these, you can use a dubbing blend that contains guard hairs; a few spiky guard hairs sticking out of the body can actually improve a caddisfly's buoyancy. You can also use muskrat, beaver, fox, Australian possum, and various synthetic dubbings. A blend of rabbit and Antron is a good material for caddisflies.

Each fly has a few individual requirements. Use a good rooster feather for the body hackle of an Elk Hair Caddis. Dry-fly saddle feathers such as those from Whiting Farms or Metz will let you make dense, very buoyant hackles on size 14 and larger caddis patterns, though you can still do a good job with top-quality neck hackles. Saddle feathers prove more economical, particularly if you tie a lot of flies. Use fine wire to counterwind the hackle; gold is the standard color, but fine fly-tying wire comes in a bunch of other colors these days, allowing you to match the color of the body. Another good choice for the rib is a piece of gel-spun polyethylene (GSP) thread such as that sold by Gudebrod; it's extremely tough and lighter than metal wire.

Elk hair comes in several natural colors, and you'll want all of them, plus some hair dyed black. The best elk hair flares under thread pressure, but not as much as deer hair does.

And speaking of pressure, you need to use thread that can produce some. On size 10, 12, and 14 flies, try tying with Ultra Thread 140, size 6/0 Uni-Thread, or size 3/0 Monocord. These are all a mite heavy for dry-fly work, but they're also strong enough to let you bear down hard on a bundle of elk hair. On size 16 and smaller flies, Flymaster 6/0, size 8/0 Uni-Thread, and similarly fine threads are okay, but only if you have soft hair and an even softer touch. Better to use something stronger.

For the wing and head of a Fathead Caddis, you need short, fine deer hair. Hair that you would use for a big Muddler might work, but it might be too hard near the tips, which is where you'll catch it with the thread. Well-stocked fly shops and catalog houses carry deer hair in a variety of lengths and textures. The material called coastal deer hair or Comparadun hair will make nice wings and heads on Fathead Caddis. When in doubt, tell the retailer what you need and ask for help.

TYING AN ELK HAIR CADDIS

The body hackle on this fly is like those of the Woolly Buggers in chapter 3, though much smaller. We'll palmer a feather from front to rear, and stitch the feather to the body with a counterwound rib spiraled from rear to front. This method reinforces the fragile hackle stem and requires us to tie down only one material, the wire, at the front of the body.

Caddisflies have fairly plump abdomens. Shape the body of a caddis pattern with several layers of dubbed thread, and make it fatter than the body of a mayfly.

Learning how much hair to use for the wing comes with experience. There's no formula; it's not as if you should always use a bundle $^X/32$ inch thick on a size 12 hook. Flies for rough water should have slightly fuller wings than those for calm streams. Elk hair varies in thickness, texture, and manageability from one patch of skin to another; an experienced tier makes adjustments. I can only advise you to avoid using too much hair, because an overly thick bundle is difficult to control and keep on top of the hook. Look at photos in books and at well-tied specimens. When in doubt, use a little less hair rather than a little more.

The tips of the hair should reach at least to the outside of the hook bend. A real caddisfly's wings extend beyond the end of its body.

Your biggest challenge is keeping the hair on top of the hook while binding it in place. Pinch the hair and the hook between your thumb and forefinger, with the tips of your fingers even with the tying thread. Pinch hard, and keep pinching while you make six tight wraps of thread. The technique is essentially that used when attaching the wing of a bucktail, except that you make each wrap in the same spot, producing a very narrow, tight band of thread. If the hair isn't held in place—firmly—while you tie it to the hook, it will certainly roll to the far side of the shank and produce a lopsided fly.

I usually trim the hackle fibers on a caddis pattern's belly to bring the body closer to the water. Cutting a broad V out of the bottom of the hackle also makes the fly more stable on the water; the wide footprint helps keep the fly from flopping onto its side as it bounces down a riffle.

Black, brown, olive, tan, cream, gold, gray, cinnamon—caddisflies come in many colors. Let's tie a cinnamon one. This pattern catches trout everywhere, particularly in the fall. Even some of the small, acidic brooks that run through the part of New England where I used to live produce good hatches of cinnamon caddis in September and October. It's a relatively large fly, which makes it easy to tie.

Hook: Standard dry fly, size 10 or 12.
Thread: Tan size 3/0 Monocord, Ultra Thread 140, or size 6/0 Uni-Thread.
Body: A blend of natural and orange rabbit fur; the color should be dirty orange, roughly like the shade of cinnamon.
Hackle: Brown.
Rib: Fine gold wire.
Wing: Natural, grayish tan elk hair. On this pattern, darker hair is better than lighter.

Body and Hackle

Tie a piece of fine gold wire to the hook. Use a piece at least 4 inches long, so that you will have something to hang on to.

Dub a plump, cigar-shaped body. Use several layers of dubbing. Leave ample room at the front of the hook—more than you'd leave for the heads of most flies.

Attach the stripped butt of the hackle feather at the front of the body. On this large specimen, I'm using a dry-fly saddle feather that will let me make a dense body hackle. On smaller flies, top-quality neck hackles work just as well.

Wind the hackle in a spiral over the body. At the rear of the body, hold the feather upright and taut, as shown.

Make a wrap with the fine wire to trap the stem of the feather against the hook. Then spiral the wire forward over the body and through the hackle, stitching the feather to the body and reinforcing the stem.

Secure the wire in front of the body. Tie down the wire with several tight wraps of thread, bend the end of the wire back, and tie down the doubled-back wire with another few wraps. Use nail clippers to cut off the excess wire.

Wing and Head

Trim the hackle fibers on top of the body. This step is optional, and the fish probably don't care whether you do it, but it makes for a neater fly.

Clean and stack a small clump of elk hair. Measure the hair against the hook. The tips of the wing should extend to at least the farthest extremity of the hook bend.

Pinch the hair in place atop the hook with your left thumb and forefinger. Hold it firmly. The procedure is exactly like that used on the bucktails in chapter 4. Bind the hair in place with at least six tight wraps of thread, each on top of the preceding one. Your goal is to produce a tight, narrow band of thread. If you trap a few hackle fibers under the wraps, as I have here, use your bodkin to free them.

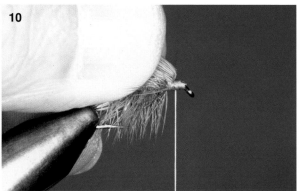

Keep the thread tight while you gently lift the butts of the hair. Hold the butts out of the way and make a few tight wraps of thread behind the hook eye.

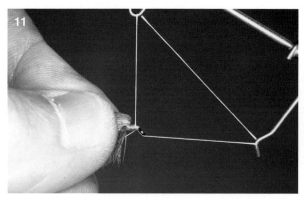

Mount your tool on the thread and make a whip-finish knot behind the hook eye. This method is easier than trying to tie off the thread on the hair; it produces a sturdier fly, too.

Clip the thread. Pinch the wing to make sure that all the hair is on top of the hook.

Cut the wing butts straight across. With your finest applicator, apply good cement to all the exposed thread wraps. Put a drop of cement on the wing butts. The homemade flexible cement described in chapter 2 is particularly good for this job.

Trimming a broad V out of the bottom of the hackle brings the body closer to the water and makes the fly more stable. Some tiers do this; some don't. I've made it a habit.

Elk Hair Caddis can be tied in an infinite variety of color schemes. Books can furnish a lot of patterns, but your own observations are the best guide. Pay attention to the colors of bugs you see while fishing. When you find a caddisfly resting on a branch, or if one lands on you, try to get a look at its underside; that's what trout see. Many caddis that look very dark from above actually have pale undersides. For that reason, natural rabbit fur, with its combination of light gray and tan, is a good body material for many caddis imitations.

Some deer hair makes excellent wings on caddis patterns. You need hair that's fairly hard, so that it doesn't flare too much when you bind it to the hook. This hair is usually finer than the stuff you would use for spinning Muddler heads, though the tips of coarse deer hair sometimes work as caddis-wing material. By and large, you will acquire caddisfly hair by accident; you'll buy a patch of deer hair that looks good for the heads of

If it doesn't flare too much, deer hair makes good caddisfly wings. A dark gray body with a black hackle and black hair is a good springtime fly on many streams.

Muddlers or hoppers, and find out at home that the hair is too stiff and hard to flare and spin. When that happens, don't throw out the patch—save it for tying Deer Hair Caddis.

In the springtime, many streams have afternoon or evening hatches of small, slender, very dark caddisflies. During such a hatch, I've done well with a size 14 or 16 pattern that has a charcoal-gray body, a black or dark grizzly hackle, and a black wing. This same fly will catch fish in late winter or early spring when the little black stoneflies hatch.

Most Elk Hair Caddis are tied for trout, but they're excellent smallmouth flies, too. If you do any fishing for river bass, tie some size 10 and even size 8 hair-wing caddis in various colors. Black flies almost always appeal to smallmouths. A caddis with a bright yellow body and a dyed-yellow grizzly hackle works well on summer days. Caddis patterns won't necessarily catch more bronzebacks than poppers will, but they let you use a lighter rod and line, and a lighter outfit makes for better sport.

TYING A FATHEAD CADDIS

It's tough to beat this fly for simplicity of construction: a dubbed body and a bundle of deer hair. Since it doesn't have a hackle, a Fathead Caddis sits low in the water, giving trout a clear view of the body. It can represent an adult caddis or an emerger stuck in the surface film. Thanks to the deer-hair wing and head, it floats very well.

This style of caddisfly has been around for a long time. I started tying Fatheads in the 1990s and loved them right away, particularly for fishing in choppy water. They draw strikes at least as well as any other type of caddis, and hook fish better than most, probably because they float in the surface film. The only drawback of this construction is that it's difficult to tie on small hooks; size 16 is about the smallest I can manage. On the other hand, Fatheads are fast and cheap to tie, since they don't require hackles.

Just about any dubbing will work for the body of a Fathead Caddis. If you use rabbit, Australian possum, or muskrat fur, leave the guard hairs in when you blend the stuff; they'll give the body a rough, spiky look. The fine-textured synthetic dubbings work fine, but there seems little point in using them to make flies that are neither sleek nor slender. Bunny fur, inexpensive and available in loads of colors, is plenty good enough for these flies.

As noted above, short, fine deer-body hair works best. Deer hair comes in many natural shades and dozens of dyed colors. Some hair has pronounced markings, and some doesn't. The more patches of hair you have, the more species of caddis your flies can imitate.

A small bundle of deer hair spins easily on a fine-wire hook. As deer-hair flies go, Fatheads are simple. But if you've never worked with deer hair, learn by tying a bunch of medium-size Marabou Muddlers (chapter 5) and then apply your new skills to smaller hooks.

Here's the generic recipe for Fathead Caddis.

Hook: Standard dry fly, sizes 10 through 16.
Thread: Size 6/0 Uni-Thread, Ultra Thread 140, 3/0 Monocord, or anything comparable; use a color that roughly matches the fly's body.
Body: Rabbit dubbing.
Wing and head: Fine deer hair; use whatever color or shade approximates the look of the caddis that you want the fly to represent.

Attach the thread about a quarter of the way back on the shank. Dub a plump body with very little taper. Leave the front of the shank bare.

Clean and stack a small bundle of deer hair. Hold the hair next to the hook; the tips should reach to at least the outside of the hook bend. Make two soft wraps of thread (no tension, that is) around the hair and the hook shank.

Tighten the wraps smoothly, not with a sudden jerk. As the hair begins to flare, release it so that it can spin around the hook. Make another few wraps through the spun hair. The procedure is exactly like the one used to make Muddler heads; see chapter 5.

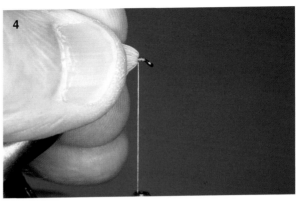

Fold the butts of the hair back. Angle the thread forward and make a few wraps around the shank in front of the hair. Whip-finish the thread while holding the hair out of the way.

Trim the head to shape. Cut off all the hair on the bottom half of the fly, leaving the hair on top. Apply a droplet of cement to the whip-finish knot.

Nothing to it, really. Tie Fatheads with cream, tan, brown, gray, cinnamon, olive, and black bodies. Some deer hair has dark bars and pronounced black tips; this stuff is good for patterns that imitate caddisflies with dark, mottled wings. Other deer hair has more subtle markings; use it to tie plainer caddis. Don't forget to make some size 14 Fatheads with dark gray bodies and black hair.

A blend of Antron dubbing and bunny fur makes a brighter body. Trout often like that, particularly on a fly that floats with its body awash. Wapsi's Life Cycle dubbings, which contain some bright synthetic fibers, make superb bodies on caddis patterns.

When it's dry, a Fathead Caddis floats like a foam strike indicator, but deer hair and dubbing fur absorb water. If you anoint the entire fly—body, wing, and head—with good floatant or treat it with a waterproofing agent such as Water Shed, a Fathead Caddis will stay on top even after catching a few trout.

A fly fisher can cover a lot of caddis hatches with the two constructions we've examined—not all of them, certainly, but most. Tying these flies draws on skills acquired by

A size 14 Fathead Caddis with an olive or tan body and a natural deer-hair wing will catch fish all season long. A black-winged fly usually represents a caddis, but it can also serve as a baby cricket.

tying other, larger patterns. Working with the components of Elk Hair and Fathead Caddis also imparts skills that apply to other, more difficult flies. Had my impatient student been willing to think this way, he might have learned how to make the Irresistibles he was so desperate to have.

The biggest advantage of tying a no-hackle dry fly is not paying for rooster feathers that cost considerably more per ounce than gold. For many tiers, that benefit outweighs the drawbacks of some no-hackle designs: marginal flotation, poor durability, difficulty of tying. When one-third of a specially bred chicken can cost more than a good fly line, fly tiers look for alternatives to fowl.

That's why I've included this chapter. The flies we're going to examine don't require hackle feathers, but they avoid the drawbacks of many no-hackle constructions. They float well, they hold up as well as most dry flies and better than some, and they're easily tied with cheap materials. I call them Spunduns, a reference to the spun deer hair that forms their wings and thoraxes.

In profile, a Spundun resembles the Comparadun style invented by Al Caucci. But the two flies are built in entirely different ways. On a Comparadun, the butts of the wing hair are bound down by thread, adding weight and bulk to the fly. The butt ends of a Spundun's deer-hair wing surround the front of the body to become a plump, buoyant thorax; they function as a miniature flotation vest. When treated with a good floatant or waterproofing agent, Spunduns float very well and for a very long time.

How long? How does five weeks grab you? That's how long a test batch of Spunduns remained afloat. Actually, they never really sank. I finally threw the flies out because after five weeks in a container of water, they began to look like a science experiment gone horribly wrong.

A Spundun has only three components: tails, body, and deer hair. It's a simple construction that progresses from one end of the hook to the other. Spunduns can be tied to represent all but the smallest mayflies, and they eliminate the expense of dry-fly hackle.

THE PARTS

As they do on most dry flies, stiff, shiny hackle fibers make good tails on Spunduns. Suitable fibers can come from large neck hackles (including those from cheap, imported rooster capes) and strung saddle feathers that don't have too much web. Other materials also work: calf tail, woodchuck guard hairs, moose mane, and, on small patterns, synthetic fibers such as Microfibbetts.

Dubbing is the most versatile body material, though Spunduns can also have bodies made with peacock herl or stripped quills. Any of the dubbings suitable for

A Spundun's excellent flotation comes from using the wing butts to make a deer-hair thorax. With only three components, these are among the simplest dry flies you can tie. They're also among the least expensive, since they don't require hackles.

other dry flies will work on a Spundun. On smaller patterns, the fine synthetic dubbings are easier to use. Natural furs should have the guard hairs removed.

Use fine, soft deer hair for the wing and thorax. Such material is usually sold as "coastal deer" or Comparadun hair. The tips of longer hair might work, but they're sometimes too hard to flare and spin when you tighten the thread. About the only way to find out is to try hair from various patches of hide.

Most deer hair has dark tips, though the length of the dark band varies considerably. Try to use hair with the shortest possible dark area at the tips. After stacking a bundle of hair, you can trim a *little* bit off the tips to shorten the dark band.

Flymaster 6/0, size 8/0 Uni-Thread, and suchlike threads are strong enough for tying small Spunduns, which require tiny bundles of deer hair. On size 14 and larger flies, I use size 3/0 Monocord or size 6/0 Uni-Thread for both their greater strength and the speed with which they let me build up the head. The latter item is important, because a Spundun's head is what props up the deer-hair wing.

TYING A MARCH BROWN SPUNDUN

There's only one tying tip for these flies: Leave the front quarter of the hook shank naked until it's time to add the deer hair. As long as you do that, you will have no trouble tying a Spundun.

For our sample fly, let's tie an Eastern March Brown version of the Spundun. This is a fairly large mayfly, which means that our imitation has enough room for me to show you another method of making divided tails. Here's the recipe.

Hook: Standard dry fly, size 12.
Thread: Tan 3/0 Monocord.
Tails: Brown or ginger hackle fibers divided by a tiny ball of dubbing.
Body: Yellowish brown dubbing. The dubbing shown in the photos is a blend of brown and yellow fur. These mayflies vary in color from place to place; some are more brown, others more yellow. If you want to duplicate the color of your local bugs, you'll have to catch some and study them. Generally, though, you can get by with a blend of two parts of medium brown material and one part of yellow. On a fly this big, rabbit fur works fine.
Wing and thorax: Natural deer hair.

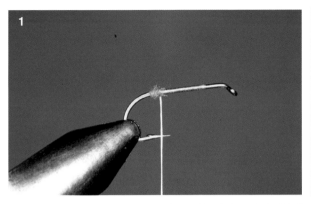

Attach the thread one-fourth of the shank length behind the hook eye; be sure to leave the first quarter of shank bare. Wrap back to the end of the shank. Twist a tiny bit of dubbing onto the thread and wrap a small ball of dubbing at the start of the hook bend.

Tie a few hackle fibers on the near side of the shank, then tie another few on the far side. The tiny ball of dubbing keeps the two bunches of fibers separated, giving the fly forked tails. You can use this trick on most mayfly patterns.

Dub the body, stopping at the one-quarter mark of the hook shank. Build the body with a slight taper.

Clean a small bundle of fine deer hair. Stack the hair to align the tips. When you separate the halves of the stacker, do it so that the tips of the hair are pointing forward, as shown.

Measure the length of the wing. The thread should intersect the hair about one hook-shank length from the tips. Hold the hair with your fingertips even with the tie-in spot. Cut the butts straight across about 1/16 inch from your fingertips. Hold the hair atop the hook and pass the thread bobbin over the hair twice, making two soft wraps around the butts.

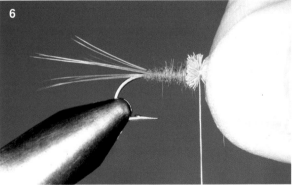

Slowly tighten the wraps by pulling the bobbin straight down. The hair will begin to flare. As the butts of the hair stand up like those in the photo, release your grip on the hair. Tighten the thread all the way, spinning the hair around the hook. Make another two or three wraps of thread in the same spot to secure the hair. The process is like spinning the head of a Muddler or Fathead Caddis, except that the hair is backward.

You can fold the hair back with your fingers, but a small tube makes the job easier. This is a piece of plastic tubing. Slide the tube over the hook eye and push it against the base of the hair. Once the hair is roughly perpendicular to the hook, you can fold it back with your fingertips.

Gather all the hair and fold it toward the rear. Wrap a head against the front of the hair. Be sure to make a number of wraps right against the base of the hair; the fly's head is all that keeps the hair elevated.

Whip-finish the thread. Trim the hair under the hook to the same length as the butts. Cement the head and apply a tiny bead of cement to the base of the wing.

The butts and the trimmed hairs form a buoyant thorax. If the pale color of the thorax bothers you, tint the hair with a permanent marker. Most mayflies, however, have pale bodies. This shot also shows the forked tails, though they're out of the camera's depth of field.

OPTIONS AND VARIATIONS

The easiest way to cook up Spundun patterns is to steal the tails and bodies of established patterns and combine them with appropriate shades of deer hair. For a Light Cahill Spundun, use the standard pattern's cream tails and body, and make the wing with pale tan deer hair. To tie a Hendrickson Spundun, swipe the tails and body of the classic dressing and spin a clump of dyed-gray hair on the front of the hook. For the wing of an Adams Spundun, use deer hair with pronounced dark bars.

You can also study real mayflies or photos to determine the best colors of deer hair to use for wings. On most patterns, though, grayish tan or dyed-gray hair works well enough to fool fish.

This construction does not lend itself to tying imitations of the smallest mayflies. I can manage Spunduns on standard size 16 dry-fly hooks; a short-shank hook lets me produce a fly roughly equivalent to one tied on a size 18 standard hook. That still leaves out some little bugs such as Tricos and the smaller olive mayflies. I can live with that. A cheap, simple, buoyant construction that I can use for better than 90 percent of mayfly hatches strikes me as a pretty good deal.

Not every Spundun needs to be a copy of a real insect. A fly tied with white hair, for instance, is easy to see in poor light or on the rough water of a riffle; it serves the same purpose as a Grizzly Riffle Fly.

If you want to tie an emerger, replace the hackle-fiber tails with a trailing shuck made of a tuft of gray polypropylene or Antron yarn. I prefer poly yarn for shucks because it's more buoyant, but I seem to be in the minority. Make the wing of an emerger slightly shorter and sparser than the wing of a dun pattern.

Water Shed is the best treatment I've found for these flies, though liquid and gel floatants also work. Anoint Spunduns with floatant before you go fishing to give the deer hair time to absorb the stuff. A reasonably waterproofed Spundun will float all day.

And won't it be nice to stop drooling over dry-fly capes that you can't afford anyway?

Create Spundun patterns by stealing the tails and bodies of proven patterns. A Light Cahill Spundun combines pale deer hair with the body and tails of the traditional dressing. Gray hair makes a good wing on a Hendickson Spundun. This construction can represent nearly any mayfly.

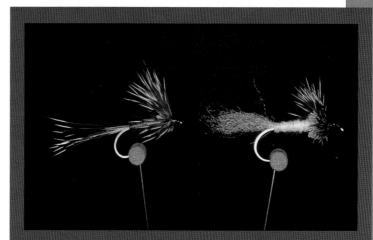

An Adams Spundun (left) can have a tail made with brown and grizzly hackle fibers or a small clump of woodchuck guard hairs. Its wing is dark, well-marked deer hair. To tie an emerger (right), substitute a tuft of poly yarn for the hackle-fiber tails and make the wing shorter than usual.

Tying flies at a fishing show invites all sorts of questions from onlookers, only some of which pertain to fly tying. People have watched me finish a fly and then asked my advice on reels, travel, waders, good places to eat lunch, and sunglasses. It's strange. I've sometimes wondered what might happen if I took a table at an angling show and hung up a sign that said, FLY-TYING DEMONSTRATIONS AND ADVICE TO THE LOVELORN. But then I decide that I probably don't want to find out.

At a show some years ago, an earnest, 20-something fly fisher watched me upholster a fishhook and then asked if he could ask a question. "Shoot," I said.

"What do you use for the Trico hatch?" was his question.

I couldn't resist. Those who lead with their chins have to take what they get.

"Cork popping bug," I said. "Black with yellow spots. On a size six Aberdeen bait hook."

The young guy didn't get it. "For *Tricos?*" he asked.

"No. For smallmouth bass," I said. Then I explained that I don't go out of my way to fish with flies that imitate plankton. God made smallmouth bass so that fishermen with sense can dodge the *Tricorythodes* hatch.

I understand that my view puts me in the barbarians' camp. That's okay; I rather like it there. Some of my best friends are barbarians.

But hatches of minibugs happen, and even we Visigoths can't always avoid them. Actually, I don't mind tying size 18 and smaller flies; it's the fishing that sometimes unhinges me. Decorating a miniature hook does strain the eyes a bit, but the mechanics of working on a small frame don't have to be complicated or even especially challenging if you follow two rules: Put fewer things and less stuff on the hook, and perform as few operations as possible at the front of the shank.

PARTS FOR TINY BUGS

My usual trout-fly threads, Danville Flymaster 6/0 and Wapsi Ultra Thread 70, work fine on the types of small flies that I tie. So do size 8/0 Uni-Thread, 8/0 or 10/0 Gudebrod thread, and similar products. Some tiers switch to extremely thin threads when they tie small flies, but I haven't found much advantage in doing so. Look at the photos in this chapter and note the heads of the flies tied to pieces of wire. Those flies are tied on little hooks, and their heads are made with Flymaster 6/0 or Ultra Thread 70.

Because of its narrow gap and minuscule spear, a tiny hook does not get a good purchase in a trout's mouth. In small sizes, some hooks have better—that is, more effective—proportions than others. Again, take a gander at the photos of flies attached to pieces of wire (that was the only way I could hold them for photography). Some of them are tied on size 18 Mustad 94840 hooks; others are built on size 22 Tiemco TMC100 hooks. You will see that the gaps of these two hooks are practically identical. But the Tiemco model has a much shorter shank, allowing me to tie a smaller fly. While I use a lot of Mustad 94840s for dry flies down to size 18, I prefer hooks with shorter shanks (but not smaller gaps) for even tinier patterns.

In the smallest sizes, the differences among competing hooks seem to become disproportionately great. There is, for instance, an obvious difference between a size 22 Mustad 94840 and a Tiemco, Daiichi, or Kamasan hook with a shank the same length; the Mustad has a smaller gap than any of those three Japanese hooks has. Since the point of the exercise is to *hook* the fish, I'd rather use the implement that does the best job—the one with the biggest gap relative to its shank length.

When you select hooks for itty-bitty flies, regard the sizes on packages as, at best, very rough guides. You want a hook with the right overall length for an imitation of a particular insect; and you want a hook with a large gap relative to that overall length.

Many tiers have trouble making small dry flies with slim, neat bodies. On really tiny patterns, you can often use the tying thread as the body material, as long as it's the right color. Size 8/0 Uni-Thread makes good-looking, reasonably durable bodies. For dubbed dry-fly bodies, use material such as Wapsi's Super Fine dubbing, which consists of extremely thin synthetic fibers. If you can find it, natural silk dubbing also makes handsome bodies on little flies. No matter what you use, don't use much of it. Half an inch of tying thread covered with the thinnest possible layer of Super Fine dubbing will make a good body on a size 18 Blue-Winged Olive. For small nymphs, use rabbit fur with all the guard hairs removed.

Two of the dry-fly constructions in this chapter have hackles. You will find that good hackle feathers greatly simplify tying small flies, mostly because premium feathers are longer and therefore easier to handle. Cheap, low-grade rooster feathers with fibers the right length for size 20 hooks are very short; trying to grab and wrap such a feather will make you crazy. Top-shelf hackle justifies its price when you tie small flies. Of course, good rooster capes cost a lot of money, which is why I've included a dry-fly construction that doesn't require hackle.

Let's look at four styles of small flies, three dry and one wet. There's no benefit in preceding them with a section about tying tips, since the tying method for each style serves the same purpose.

WINGLESS DRYS

When I was a kid, most fly fishers called this type of fly a midge. Although these simple, three-part flies will often take fish during a hatch of true midges, they're not imitations of those little insects. A real midge has no tails, and it carries its wings flat over its body. With its tails and hackle collar, this construction looks more like a small mayfly. But the "midge" label persists among many anglers, even though we also have scores of other designs that represent genuine midges.

There's not much to one of these flies: tails, dubbed body, and a few turns of hackle. They catch fish, and that makes them good enough for me. I used to know an accomplished dry-fly fisherman who maintained that all wings on all dry flies are decorations added to make the lures more appealing to the anglers who buy them. Large or small, none of this gent's dry flies had wings, and yet he caught loads of trout in heavily pressured streams. The wing argument, however, is best left for a long evening in a comfortable tavern that stocks good whiskey.

Omitting wings eliminates one of the difficulties of tying on small frame. We can get rid of another problem by wrapping the hackle backward—from front to back, that is. A tiny hook has very little room for securing and trimming materials at the front of the shank. By winding the hackle from front to back, we don't have to tie down or trim anything in the tiny space behind the hook eye.

For our sample fly, let's use an old pattern generally called a Gray Midge or Grizzly Midge. It will take fish during a hatch of any of the small, dark mayflies—Tricos, tiny blue quills, and so forth. I've used it to catch trout eating small olives. While it's not a good representation of a true midge, it often works during hatches of them, too. Here's the recipe.

Hook: Any dry-fly hook, size 18 to as small as you can handle.
Thread: Black.
Tails: A few fibers from a grizzly or dark dun hackle.
Body: Gray Super Fine dubbing or something similar.
Hackle: Grizzly.

Simple, wingless patterns catch trout and relieve some of the headaches of tying small flies. Note that these hooks have similar gaps, but that the one on the left has a shorter shank than the other two.

My camera equipment does not permit me to shoot good photos of tying steps on a size 18 hook; I simply can't get close enough to fill much of the frame with the fly. So, the hook in the step-by-step photos is a size 12. The three flies attached to the piece of wire are tied on tiny hooks.

Wrap a base of thread on the hook. Attach a few hackle fibers at the end of the shank. Bind down the butts of the tail fibers, and then attach the butt end of the hackle feather slightly behind the hook eye, leaving room for the fly's head. Attach the feather with an X-wrap of thread so that it's roughly perpendicular to the hook, and then bind the stripped stem along the shank.

Twist a tiny bit of dubbing onto the tying thread and make the fly's body. Dub the body all the way up to the hackle feather, but then bring the thread back to the rear of the thorax area. Note where the thread is hanging in this photo; that's where you want it before you start wrapping the hackle.

Wrap the hackle from front to rear. On a small hook, you will make only a few wraps. Hold the feather taut and make one wrap with the tying thread to trap the feather's stem against the hook.

Wind the thread forward through the hackle collar, stitching the stem of the feather to the hook. With the tips of your finest scissors, clip the excess feather at the rear of the collar. There's nothing to secure or trim at the front of the fly—all you have to do is whip-finish the thread.

Tied in various colors, these simple little flies will catch trout during many hatches of small mayflies. Besides the gray version, tie some with olive bodies and dun hackles. For a Sulfur pattern, use a size 16 hook, cream tails and hackle, and yellowish cream dubbing. A cream body with dun tails and a dun hackle makes a passable imitation of a pale evening dun or pale morning dun.

POST-WING DUNS

Do wings improve a tiny dry fly? I don't know. I can't recall having caught a trout simply because I switched from a wingless to a winged pattern, but I know better than to extrapolate from my own experience with small flies. Many anglers who fish small flies more often and more seriously than I do say that wings make a big difference.

Of one thing I'm certain: Tying upright, divided wings on a size 18 or 20 hook does not top my list of favorite amusements. I can do it, but not without violating a Commandment. Adding wings can also add too much bulk and weight to a small fly. Elegant, lifelike wings don't do anything for you if they make the body unacceptably fat or impair the fly's flotation. But real insects have wings.

On a small fly (these are all size 18), a tuft of polypropylene yarn strikes a compromise between no wings and a pair of wings. These flies are rugged and easy to tie, and trout like them.

The easiest solution is to split the difference and think singular rather than plural. Instead of wings, give a small dry fly a wing, a post like those on the parachute flies described in chapter 9. A poly-yarn post suggests the wings of a mayfly at rest, adds no bulk to the hook, and doesn't make a small fly much more difficult to tie.

Let's tie a Post-Wing Olive to see how this method works. Here's the parts list.

Hook: Any dry-fly hook size 18 or smaller.
Thread: Olive.
Tails: Dun hackle fibers.
Wing post: Gray polypropylene yarn.
Body: Fine, soft, olive dubbing such as Wapsi Super Fine. Olive mayflies come in various shades, but a brownish olive body usually satisfies trout.
Hackle: Medium to dark dun.

Attach a few hackle fibers at the end of the hook shank and bind down their butts. About a third of shank length behind the eye, attach a thin piece of poly yarn across the hook with two X-wraps of thread.

Pull the ends of the yarn upright. Make a few wraps of thread around the base of the post to gather all the fibers together. Attach the butt end of the hackle feather between the base of the post and the hook eye. If you can manage it, use an X-wrap to tie the feather across the shank, and then bind the stem along the side of the hook. Ideally, you will have a tiny bit of space between the hackle feather and the wing post, as this fly does. Be sure to leave room for the fly's head in front of the hackle.

Twist a wee bit of dubbing onto the thread and make the fly's body. Take one wrap of dubbed thread in front of the post, and then bring the thread behind the post. Note the position of the thread in this photo; this is about where you want it before you wrap the hackle.

Wrap the hackle from front to rear. On a small hook, you will probably have room for three wraps—one in front of the post and two behind. Hold the hackle feather taut above the fly, and make one wrap of thread to trap the stem against the hook. Then wind the thread forward through the hackle and whip-finish it behind the hook eye.

Tie off the thread. With your fine scissors, clip the leftover tip of the hackle feather. Trim the poly-yarn wing to length.

This construction is a good one for middling-small flies such as Sulfurs and Pale Evening Duns. A size 16 fly looks skimpy without wings, but the hook doesn't have much room for tricky operations. The poly-yarn post strikes a happy compromise. Gray posts look more like the wings of real mayflies, but a fly with a white post is easier to see in dim light. To make one of these flies resemble a parachute pattern, simply trim the hackle fibers beneath the hook.

NO-HACKLE HAIRWINGS

Hackled flies have one drawback: the price of good rooster plumage. After springing for dun, cream, and grizzly Grade 2 capes (the bare minimum that he needs for small flies), a tier might find himself $150 poorer.

Little flies, however, don't need much help to float. A wing of buoyant deer or elk hair will keep a size 18 or 20 pattern on the surface and let it float with its body in the surface film rather than above it. This style of fly is nothing more than a hair-wing caddis minus the body hackle. Add tails, and the same construction can serve as a small mayfly, as you'll see in a minute.

You need soft, short, fine hair for the wings of these flies. Deer generally works better than elk, though some patches of elk hair have tips sufficiently fine and springy. If you don't have much experience buying deer hair, ask for help at the fly shop. If you can find it, dyed-gray deer hair is ideal for the wings of mayfly patterns. For caddis, you'll want natural hair in several shades.

Since tying this type of fly involves bearing down on a clump of hair, don't use extra-thin thread. You want the strength of standard 6/0 or 8/0 thread.

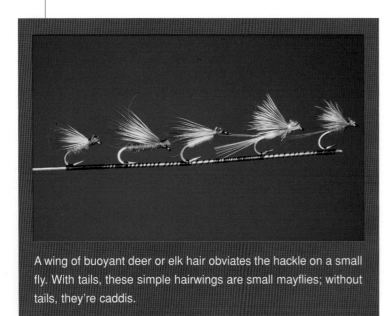

A wing of buoyant deer or elk hair obviates the hackle on a small fly. With tails, these simple hairwings are small mayflies; without tails, they're caddis.

Another olive pattern will serve as a demonstration. You will need the following materials.

Hook: Any dry-fly hook size 18 or smaller.
Thread: Olive 6/0 or 8/0.
Tails: A few dun hackle fibers.
Body: Olive dubbing.
Wing: A small clump of fine deer hair. Hair dyed light gray is ideal, but natural hair will generally satisfy the fish. The wing should be about as long as the hook shank.

Attach the tails and dub the body. Leave the first quarter of the hook shank bare. If you don't leave enough room at the front of the hook, you won't be able to make the wing.

Cut and clean a small clump of deer hair. On a size 18 hook, use a bundle of hair about the thickness of the lead in a standard No. 2 pencil. Stack the hair to even the tips. Hold the hair atop the hook to establish the length of the wing. Pinch both the hair and the hook shank between the tips of your thumb and forefinger, and bind the hair in place with several snug wraps of thread.

Carefully lift the butts of the hair and make a few wraps of thread behind the hook eye. Whip-finish the thread behind the eye; the procedure is exactly the same as that used on the Elk Hair Caddis in chapter 10. Cut the wing butts. Before applying head cement, try to coax a couple of hairs on each side down, so that they will act as outriggers; tweezers help with this job. Cement the wing butts and the exposed thread.

Tie a caddis version the same way, but without tails. Make the wing of a caddis slightly longer than the hook. Black, cream, olive, and tan are good colors for the bodies of no-hackle caddisflies.

ITTY-BITTY NYMPHS

A fly fisher's need for small nymphs depends on where he fishes. When I lived in Vermont, I used to fish several streams that contained a good variety of fish food but didn't produce overwhelming numbers of any single type of bug. If I stumbled on trout rising to an autumn hatch of blue-winged olives, I'd cast an appropriately small fly. But I never fished a little olive nymph unless I saw the insects on the water and trout feeding on them. Some years, I never had to cast a nymph smaller than size 14 because my times on the water never coincided with good hatches of small mayflies. If the trout weren't eating blue-winged olives right at the moment, they were just as likely to take a size 12 foam ant as a size 18 nymph.

In other places, small nymphs get a lot more action. If a stream produces hatch after hatch of little insects, trout get used to eating them. On such a river, an angler would do well with a tiny nymph.

You can make very good small nymphs by tying stripped-down versions of their larger cousins. Little hooks don't have room for enough weighting wire to make a difference, so don't bother adding any; if you need to get deep, pinch a small split shot on the leader. To keep the bodies neat and sleek, dub them with bunny fur from which most of the guard hairs have been removed. If you want a small nymph to have a rib, make it with fine wire or a single strand of pearlescent Flashabou instead of the oval tinsel you'd use on a size 12 pattern. Don't try to tie down the wing case *and* add two clumps of hackle fibers behind the eye of a size 16 or 18 hook; make the nymph's legs by picking out a few fibers on each side of the thorax.

The two olive nymphs are tied on standard-length wet-fly hooks. Although they're shorter, they have the same gaps as the 1X-long nymph hooks used for the Sulfur Nymph (second from left) and Pale Little Nymph. All four flies are stripped-down versions of larger constructions.

I will use 1X-long nymph hooks down to size 16. For a nymph shorter than that, I prefer a standard-length wet-fly hook. In other words, I'll use a size 16 wet-fly hook rather than a size 18 nymph hook. Those two chassis are roughly the same overall length, but the wet-fly hook has a bigger gap and longer point, which make for a better purchase in a trout's yap. It's also a tad heavier than the nymph hook.

Except for those changes, tying a small nymph is just like tying one of the rabbit-fur nymphs described in chapter 6. That chapter has a recipe for olive nymphs; here are a couple more patterns.

Sulfur Nymph

Hook: 1X-long nymph, size 16.

Thread: Tan or reddish brown.

Tails: Ginger or tan hackle fibers.

Abdomen: Tan rabbit fur with a tiny bit of orange blended in.

Rib (optional): Pearl Flashabou.

Wing case: A slip from a goose or duck quill.

Thorax: The same dubbing used for the abdomen.

Pale Little Nymph

Hook: 1X-long nymph or standard wet fly, size 16.

Thread: Tan or gray.

Tails: Dun hackle fibers.

Abdomen: Natural rabbit fur.

Rib (optional): Pearl Flashabou.

Wing case: A slip from a goose or duck quill.

Thorax: The same dubbing used for the abdomen.

I have seen exquisite little imitations of blue-winged olive and *Tricorythodes* duns tied with cut wings, segmented abdomens, and perfectly divided tails. I've even tied a few size 20 cut-wing patterns, just to see if I could. But I have no desire to fill a box with such flies. Simple constructions usually work fine when trout are eating tiny insects. Indeed, if there's ever a time when how you fish matters more than what you cast, it's when you use small flies. And if minibugs, 7X tippets, and neurotic trout get on your nerves, you can always sling a cork popper (black with yellow spots) at smallmouth bass. A few hours of bass fishing restore one's perspective.

One of the most popular flies of our time might also be one of the most misunderstood. Maybe it's more accurate to say that many anglers see only part of the beauty of Bob Clouser's Deep Minnow design. When Lefty Kreh introduced Deep Minnows to the fly-fishing world in an article for *Fly Fisherman* magazine in the late 1980s, a fair number of anglers either praised or blasted the flies for their allegedly jiglike characteristics.

"This is a great fly," said some. "Thanks to its dumbbell eyes, it has a deadly jigging action that fish can't resist."

"These things aren't flies," said others. "They're merely jigs that heathens can throw with fly rods."

Neither extreme is right. Whether they love or hate Deep Minnows, folks who use the "fly-rod jig" label don't know much about jigs. It's practically impossible to impart a true jigging action to any lure with a fly-fishing outfit. Real jigs dart upward and then plummet very rapidly. The action comes from the movement of the rod, and one cannot replicate it with a 9-foot fly rod and 50 feet of fat fly line retrieved by stripping. A Deep Minnow doesn't have a genuine jigging action; rather, it takes a sinuous path as it swims, rising and falling in a series of curves. It is a nose-heavy, upside-down bucktail, and its movements are much less abrupt than those of, say, a rubber-skirted, ½-ounce spider jig manipulated by a bass fisherman.

Fans and critics of Deep Minnows are fixated on the dumbbell eyes. Yes, one can make a smallmouth-size Deep Minnow with a dumbbell so heavy that the fly cannot be cast with anything lighter than a tarpon outfit. But "weighted" doesn't have to mean "tied with as much lead as possible," and a Deep Minnow doesn't have to weigh a ton to work. Even on a large specimen, a small dumbbell will do the job.

Nor are these strictly deepwater flies. Sure, they'll sink faster than a standard Mickey Finn, mostly because of the location of the weight rather than the amount. But a lightly weighted Deep Minnow, one tied with a small dumbbell or a piece of bead chain, is an excellent bucktail for shallow water. They've become popular on the bonefish flats.

The beauty of Clouser's invention lies in how the pieces work together. Since all the weight is near the front, the fly tips nose-down during a pause in the retrieve. That lets it sink more quickly than a Muddler or Woolly Bugger that might weigh just as much. Its nose-heavy design also gives the fly more vertical movement than any conventional bucktail has. The flash is where it should be in a baitfish imitation, along the center of the fly. And, of course, a Deep Minnow swims with its hook up, dodging many of the hazards that snag other flies.

Fly-rod jigs? Not quite. With all their weight up front, Deep Minnows swim with a sinuous movement, but they don't have a true jigging action. And they don't have to be very heavy to work.

A Deep Minnow is not a difficult construction, but it does present a couple of durability challenges. Many tiers have trouble attaching dumbbell eyes so that they stay put. Others paint the eyes with finishes that chip off within half a dozen casts. Some tiers fail to protect the band of thread that secures the belly hair behind the eyes, and their flies fall apart after a few fish.

We'll lick those challenges and tie a very rugged, good-looking Deep Minnow right after taking a quick look at the components.

THE PARTS

Most Deep Minnows are tied on standard-length hooks with straight eyes. For saltwater patterns, most tiers use O'Shaughnessy hooks such as the Mustad 3407 (tinned) or 34007 (stainless). A tinned or bronzed O'Shaughnessy hook is also a good chassis for a freshwater Deep Minnow, but freshwater tiers have the option of using lighter hooks such as Mustad's 3366, a Sproat-bend model. Nymph hooks also work; a size 6 or 8, 2X-long nymph iron makes a good frame for a small, light Deep Minnow intended for panfish or trout.

Think about the hooks you use for these flies. There's a considerable difference in weight between a size 2 saltwater hook, which is made of stout stuff, and a size 2 Mustad 3366, which is made of much lighter wire. Even with a small, light dumbbell, a Deep Minnow tied on a 3366 will flip over in the water and swim with its point up. The heavier saltwater iron might need a bigger dumbbell to counterbalance the weight of its bend and spear. Under the best circumstances, these flies are not an unalloyed joy to cast. Why throw any more weight than you have to? Select hooks and dumbbells according to the depth you need to achieve.

Lead remains the most common material for dumbbell eyes, but dumbbells are also made of brass, tin, and aluminum. Lead, of course, is the most dense of these materials, but that's not always an advantage. A $\frac{1}{50}$-ounce lead dumbbell is smaller than a $\frac{1}{50}$-ounce dumbbell made of tin or brass. The tin or brass weight, then, will make larger eyes on the fly, and most anglers regard big eyes as a good thing on a baitfish pattern. The aluminum Deep See eyes made by Spirit River are positively huge compared to lead dumbbells of the same weight. So, if you want Deep Minnows with extra-large eyes, you don't necessarily have to make extra-heavy flies.

How heavy a dumbbell to use depends on the size of the hook, the depth of the water where you will use the fly, the speed of the current, and whether you plan to use a floating or sinking-tip line. You probably need less weight than you think. In fresh water, a $\frac{1}{50}$-ounce dumbbell is often heavy enough, even with a size 1 or 2 Sproat hook. Unless you want to dredge the bottom of a reservoir, you'll probably never need a Deep Minnow tied with a dumbbell heavier than $\frac{1}{36}$ ounce. Fishing with a sinking-tip line reduces the amount of weight you need to build into your flies. If you use a floating line, attach the fly to the tippet with a loop knot rather than a clinch knot; the loop makes it easier for the fly to tip nose-down and sink.

If you've been tying freshwater Deep Minnows with $\frac{1}{36}$- or $\frac{1}{24}$-ounce dumbbells, try making a few with lighter eyes. You'll probably find that they still sink deep enough. Bead-chain eyes work fine on smaller flies, those from size 4 down.

Since I build Deep Minnows in stages, I use two types of thread: a middleweight or heavy thread to attach the eyes to the hook, and a fine thread to tie the fly. For mounting the eyes, I use white size 3/0 Monocord, 140-denier Ultra Thread, Flat Waxed Nylon, or Flymaster Plus, depending on the size of the fly. For the hair and flash material, I generally use 6/0 Flymaster or 70-denier Ultra Thread, but any fine thread will work.

Bucktail is the standard material for the belly and back. Fine hair is easier to use and livelier in the water than coarse bucktail. On a size 6 or smaller fly, you can use calf tail, squirrel tail, or kid hair. Fox tail, particularly arctic fox tail, with some of the underfur removed makes a very lively Deep Minnow.

A combination of Flashabou and Krystal Flash seems to work better than either material by itself. Likewise, a mix of colors seems more appealing to fish than one color. For instance, on the ubiquitous chartreuse-and-white Deep Minnow, try combining silver Flashabou and Krystal Flash with some pearlescent material. A mix of pearl, silver, light green, and pink replicates the colors of many baitfish.

TYING TIPS

Even when they're attached with a zillion tight wraps of thread, dumbbell and bead-chain eyes can twist out of alignment. The solution isn't another zillion wraps, but a hard, solid foundation made by bonding the thread to the hook. Superglue to the rescue. Wind an open spiral of strong thread over most of the hook shank. Coat the spiral with superglue, and then, while the glue is still wet, wrap another layer or two of thread. As the superglue cures, it will bond these layers of the thread to the hook.

Attach the dumbbell slightly forward of the midpoint of the shank. Secure it with a combination of **X**-wraps and diagonal wraps made with tight thread. Apply superglue to the wraps, particularly where they go around the hook shank. Eyes mounted this way generally stay put.

Fly shops sell dumbbells that are specially machined to accept stick-on plastic eyes, but such fancy components are too pricey for my tastes. My stinginess leaves me with the problem of painting plain lead or tin eyes. Vinyl jig paint does a much better job than fly-tying lacquers, model-car enamels, or nail polish, all of which chip easily when applied over lead. Vinyl paint sticks to lead fairly well, and it remains slightly flexible after it cures. If you're going to paint the eyes on Deep Minnows, don't bother with anything but vinyl jig paint. You can get it from companies that sell lure-making supplies; Jann's Netcraft is one. You'll need white, a color for the irises (red, yellow, and orange are good), clear, and black. Get some thinner, too, and add it to the paints as necessary.

Give the ends of the dumbbell a base coat of white. It will dry in about 10 minutes, at which time you can apply a coat of red, yellow, orange, or whatever. Let the color coat dry, and then cover the entire dumbbell with at least one coat of clear vinyl. Apply the black pupils last. *Do not* paint the pupils and then apply the clear coat—the clear paint will soften the pupils and make them run.

Obviously, this is not a method suited to tying one fly at a time. Tie Deep Minnows in stages. Fasten dumbbells to a bunch of hooks, and then paint all the eyes. Use wooden clothespins to hold the hooks while the paint dries, or stick the hooks into a block of plastic foam.

Go easy with the hair. Like conventional bucktails, Deep Minnows should be sparse. The fly in the sequence below is dressed about as heavily as a Deep Minnow should be.

These flies don't have carved-in-stone proportions, but try to use hair that's at least three times the length of the hook. The shorter the hair relative to the length of the hook, the less up-and-down action the fly will have.

THREE-STAGE MINNOWS

Besides eyes that twist out of alignment, some Deep Minnows have another durability problem. If it's not cemented, the band of thread that secures the belly hair behind the eyes will abrade in a hurry. Once that band of thread falls apart, the fly loses its shape.

The solution is to protect that band of thread behind the dumbbell. As you'll see in a minute, we'll use an unusual, two-bobbin method to attach the belly hair, and we'll protect all the thread with cement before proceeding with the rest of the fly. And since we'll use two bobbins, we'll load the rear one with red thread. That way, the band of thread behind the eyes not only secures the belly hair, but also suggests a minnow's gills.

This approach isn't as time-consuming as it might seem. Tying production-line style is very efficient, and in this case it produces a more durable fly. If a fly lasts longer in the field, I don't mind investing an extra two minutes at the vise.

Believe it or not, Deep Minnows come in colors other than chartreuse and white. Let's tie one that represents a variety of fresh- and saltwater baitfish—chubs, shiners, herring, baby bunker, silversides, and others. Here's what you'll need.

Hook: Mustad 3366, size 1 or 2. If you want a saltwater fly, substitute a tinned or stainless hook.
Threads: Three altogether—white Flymaster Plus to attach the eyes, any red thread for the band that secures the belly hair behind the eyes, and gray 6/0 or 8/0 for the nose.
Eyes: A $1/50$ or $1/36$-ounce dumbbell painted with vinyl jig paint.
Belly: White bucktail.
Flash: Holographic silver Flashabou, silver Krystal Flash, pearlescent Flashabou, and pearlescent Krystal Flash. Use only four to six strands of each.
Back: Gray bucktail topped with a little hair from the brown portion of the tail.

Eyes

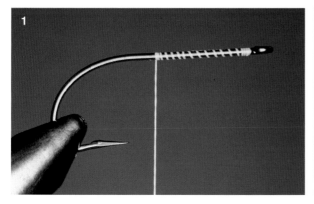

Attach the thread behind the eye of the hook and wrap a spiral over two-thirds to three-quarters of the shank. Apply a smear of superglue to the spiral of thread.

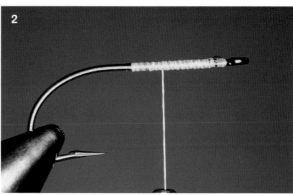

Wrap a layer of thread forward over the wet superglue. Reverse direction and wrap to about the middle of the shank. The superglue will bond the thread to the hook.

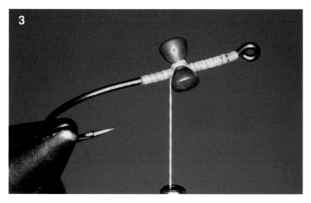

Attach the dumbbell with a few X-wraps of thread as shown here. Make sure that it's straight, and then secure it by wrapping diagonally in one direction and then the other. Keep the thread tight as you wrap. Finish with a few more X-wraps.

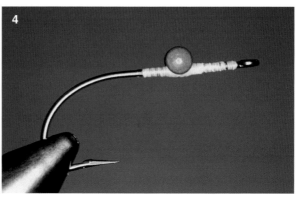

Whip-finish the thread and cut it. Check the alignment of the eyes one more time, and then coat all the thread wraps with superglue.

Belly

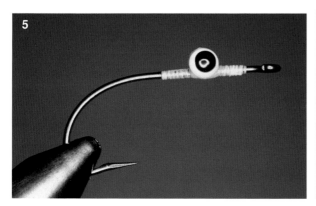

Give the eyes a coat of white vinyl jig paint. Let the white paint dry, and apply a coat of yellow or red. After that dries, give the entire dumbbell a coat of clear vinyl jig paint. Let the clear coat dry most of the way, and then apply the black pupils.

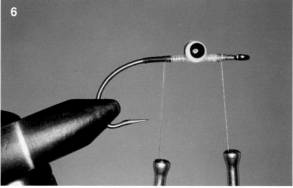

You need two bobbins for this operation. Load one with red thread and the other with whatever color you want to use for the nose of the fly. Attach the red thread behind the eyes. Tie on with the other thread at the front of the shank.

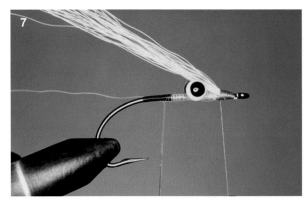

Attach a sparse clump of white bucktail at the front of the hook. Trim the butt ends and bind them down.

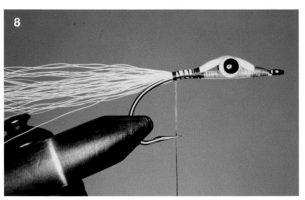

Whip-finish and clip the front thread. Pull the hair down behind the eyes and secure it with the red thread.

Flash and Back

Wrap a band of red thread. Whip-finish and cut the thread. Give the red band two coats of good head cement or one coat of superglue. Let the cement dry.

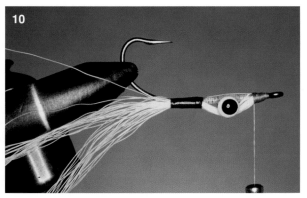

Invert the hook and reattach the nose thread.

Tie on the flash material. The flashy stuff should be at least as long as the bucktail.

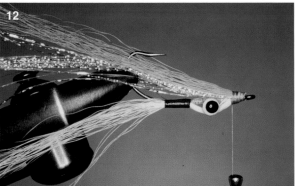

Attach a sparse clump of bucktail (gray, on this fly). Trim the butts, give them a drop of cement, and bind them down.

This step is optional, but it adds a nice touch. Cut a very small bundle of hair from the brown portion of the bucktail. Tie this dark hair on top of the previous bunch. Note that the dark hair is shorter than the material beneath it. Trim the butts, bind them down, and finish the fly's nose.

Cement the fly's nose, allowing a little cement to run back into the butts of the bucktail. On the finished fly, the band of red thread suggests a baitfish's gills. Since all of the thread has been cemented, the fly will hold up very well.

OPTIONS AND VARIATIONS

Fly tiers make Deep Minnows in every imaginable color scheme, and they catch fish with all of them. Saltwater anglers have been particularly creative in cooking up new versions of this design, and I have nothing to add to their contributions. My only observation is that a lot of freshwater anglers still don't appreciate the value of small—tiny, even—Deep Minnows. A Deep Minnow tied on a size 8 nymph hook and with an extra-small dumbbell or small bead-chain eyes is a deadly panfish and trout fly. It's no harder to cast than, say, a weighted Muddler or Woolly Bugger, but it snags much less often.

In sizes smaller than 6, standard-length hooks don't have enough room to permit the construction of a good Deep Minnow. Even a size 6 is often marginal. That's why I use 1X- or, more often, 2X-long nymph hooks for the smallest versions of these flies. The longer shank has enough room for me to mount the eyes and tie down the belly hair. And a nymph hook's turned-down eye (which becomes a turned-up eye with this type of fly) helps a baby Deep Minnow flip over in the water, which lets

A three-stage construction method produces a Deep Minnow with superior durability and a band of red thread that represents a baitfish's gills. This is a size 4 Deep Sculpin pattern tied for smallmouths or large trout.

me use lighter eyes. Small Aberdeen jig hooks are also good, especially if you want to tie miniature Deep Minnows for crappies, perch, or bluegills.

Either an extra-small dumbbell or a piece of bead chain will work on a size 8 Deep Minnow. I like bead chain because the holes in the outboard sides of the beads look like

Small Deep Minnows tied on size 6 or 8 nymph hooks are first-rate flies for crappies, perch, big bluegills, and trout. Bead-chain eyes add enough weight to one of these little bucktails.

pupils. When I do use tiny dumbbells, I don't bother to paint them; there's simply not enough room to get artistic.

Since these flies are only a couple of inches long, you can tie them with calf tail, squirrel tail, kid goat, or fox tail. Panfish don't require fancy flies. Perch, bluegills, and crappies will eat white, yellow, and chartreuse Deep Minnows with a little pearlescent Krystal Flash or Angel Hair sandwiched between the layers of hair.

For trout, try gray over white, tan over white, olive over white, gray squirrel tail over white, and olive over yellow, all with pearlescent flash material. If you fish in streams that have a lot of sculpins or darters, try this Deep Sculpin pattern.

Deep Sculpin

Hook: 2X-long nymph, size 6 or 8.
Eyes: Brass bead chain.
Threads: White or yellow to attach the eyes; red and brown for the hair.
Belly: Yellow or tan calf tail.
Flash: A mix of gold Flashabou and gold Krystal Flash.
Back: Red or fox squirrel tail.

The beauty of that fly is that you can pitch it across the current or slightly upstream, throw an upstream mend to let it plummet to the bottom, and then bounce it along the streambed without too much risk of hanging up. It's actually more pleasant to cast than a Muddler tied with a couple of inches of lead wire under the body.

Trout will eat some sizable minnows—I once cleaned a 10-inch brookie that had a brace of 3-inch minnows in its stomach—so you might also want a few Deep Minnows tied on standard size 4 hooks. Bead-chain eyes will work fine on these, too, unless you fish in deep, fast water, where you might want a small dumbbell. And if one of your purist buddies derides your Deep Minnows as "fly-rod jigs," tell him that he understands neither jigs nor these marvelous flies.

The problem with fish, besides their occasional inability to recognize the excellence of our flies, is their fondness for weed beds, sunken timber, rock piles, submerged brush, dock pilings, and other hazards. Fish live near and among snags, and catching them entails risking the loss of some flies. Finding ways to lessen that risk—that is, to make flies more or less snag resistant—not only reduces the number of flies sacrificed to hazards, but also lets an angler fish more aggressively and daringly. A well-rounded fly tier knows several ways to make his flies snag resistant.

Many anglers have no choice but to deal with snags. A largemouth bass or pike fisherman who avoids weeds and drowned timber also avoids the fish. Bonefish anglers strip their flies across flats covered with turtle grass, and redfish anglers must contend with both grass and oyster beds. A fly fisher after smallmouths has to retrieve his flies over piles of stones or along crevices in a rocky bottom.

Most trout fishermen don't tie snag-resistant flies, but they should. Trout like weed beds for the same reasons that other fish do: A patch of thick weeds is a good hunting ground and hiding spot. Brown and brook trout gravitate toward sunken trees. A trout angler who avoids hazards also misses a lot of opportunities.

Fewer hang-ups equals more fish. Learning how to construct a few snag-resistant flies will make any angler's time on the water more productive and enjoyable.

BEND-BACKS

The easiest way to make a baitfish pattern snag resistant is to build it so that it swims with the hook up. This is one of the advantages of Bob Clouser's Deep Minnow design: The fly's dumbbell eyes overbalance the hook and make it ride with the point up, away from most snags. Deep Minnows, of course, were not the first flies tied this way. Bonefish anglers have long tied upside-down flies weighted with pieces of bead chain.

The old Bend-Back style of bucktail also swims upside down, but it doesn't need any extra weight to do it. That's good, because sometimes you don't want or need to cast a pattern tied with a dumbbell or section of bead chain. You can swim an unweighted Bend-Back over the top of a

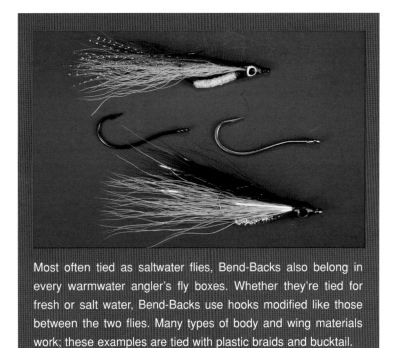

Most often tied as saltwater flies, Bend-Backs also belong in every warmwater angler's fly boxes. Whether they're tied for fresh or salt water, Bend-Backs use hooks modified like those between the two flies. Many types of body and wing materials work; these examples are tied with plastic braids and bucktail.

shallow weed bed or along an oyster bar, or let a slow current swing it across the rocky bottom of a smallmouth river. When the wind blows, you'll find an unweighted Bend-Back a lot easier to cast than a Deep Minnow.

These days, most fly fishers think of Bend-Backs as saltwater flies, but I'm reasonably sure that the idea came from freshwater bass fishing. No matter where they originated, Bend-Backs are excellent bucktails that catch fish in every environment from grassy red-fish flats to weedy bass ponds to rocky trout streams.

As the name suggests, tying one of these flies begins with bending the hook, which is usually a standard-length, straight-eye O'Shaughnessy model such as a Mustad 3407 or a Sproat model such as a Mustad 3366. Bend the shank away from the point, and bend it just a little; a pronounced bend will make the hook less efficient at hooking fish. I've long used an old, well-worn adjustable wrench for bending hooks, though smooth-jawed pliers also work. Make the bend far enough behind the hook eye so that you will have a section of straight shank long enough for the fly's head.

Once you've bent the hook, tie an upside-down bucktail on it. Make the body with tinsel, plastic braid, Mylar tubing, flashy chenille such as Ice Chenille or Estaz, plain chenille, or yarn. I generally construct the body with the hook in the conventional, point-down position in my vise, and then turn the hook over to attach the wing; some other tiers start with the hook upside down.

You can use any number of materials for the wings of Bend-Backs. Bucktail, calf tail, squirrel tail, kid goat, and various synthetics all work. Add some Flashabou or Krystal Flash if you want, either along the sides of the wing or sandwiched between layers of hair. Give the fly painted or stick-on eyes.

Bend-Backs do not have standard proportions or established patterns. You can tie them pretty much however you like, making them as plain or fancy as you please. Any thread will work. Braid, tubing, or plastic chenille makes a more substantial body than flat tinsel does. A two-tone wing—brown bucktail over white bucktail, say, or olive over white or yellow—makes for a more convincing baitfish imitation. Generally, you should make the wing at least twice as long as the hook. Don't get carried away with flash material; a few pieces of Krystal Flash or Flashabou will do.

Like standard bucktails, Bend-Backs will catch nearly anything. Saltwater fishermen build them on stainless-steel hooks as large as size 3/0; panfish anglers use Mustad 3366 hooks as small as size 6 to tie Bend-Backs for crappies or white perch. Large or small, Bend-Backs dodge most snags.

Any fly tied on an inverted hook *must* have its barb mashed down. Upside-down flies often hook fish in the roofs of their mouths, where a barbed hook can leave a nasty wound. Please make sure that all your Bend-Backs, Deep Minnows, and other flies that swim with their points up are barbless.

UPSIDE-DOWN MUDDLERS

A Marabou Muddler is too good a streamer to remain in your fly box just because you're afraid of losing it. Tying the fly upside down on a specially weighted hook makes it relatively snagproof, letting you pitch it into deadfalls and other hazardous spots.

The first step is attaching all the weight on one side of the hook shank. Double a piece of weighting wire to make a slug slightly longer than half the length of the hook shank, and tie the doubled wire on the side of the shank away from the point—the side that's usually the top, that is. Prepare another, shorter piece of doubled wire and bind it atop the first slug. These pieces of wire will function as a keel weight. Cement the thread wraps with superglue.

After the glue dries, turn the hook over in your vise and tie a Marabou Muddler. A plastic braid such as Wapsi's Sparkle Braid works best for making the body. The fly's wing goes on the same side of the shank as the bend and point. Trim the head flat on the bottom, and clip off the hairs on the belly side of the fly.

For smallmouths, largemouths, trout, pickerel, pike, and panfish, upside-down Marabou Muddlers are excellent streamers that rarely hang up on weeds or brush. Like conventional Muddlers, inverted specimens work especially well in stained or dirty water; their bulky heads push a lot of water, creating turbulence that fish can detect with their lateral lines. For bass fishing in off-color water or at night, a big, black, upside-down Marabou Muddler is tough to beat. In clear water, use patterns tied in baitfish colors.

INVERTED NYMPHS

Nymphs, too, can be made to swim with their hook points up, though few tiers make them this way. That seems a strange oversight, since nymphs are particularly prone to hanging up on the beds of rivers and streams.

Like tying a Bend-Back, constructing an inverted nymph begins with modifying the hook. In this case, though, you want to bend the front of the shank *toward* the hook point. Use a 2X- or 3X-long hook of the appropriate length. For instance, if you'd normally tie

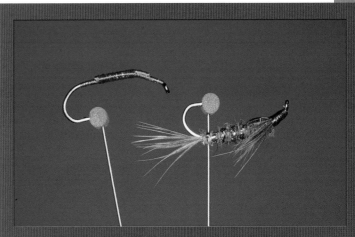

An upside-down Marabou Muddler will elude most hazards. Before tying the fly, use doubled pieces of weighting wire to make a keel weight on the hook.

A nymph is less likely to snag on the riverbed if it's tied on a 2X-long hook bent and weighted like the one at the top. Note the weight distribution: a strip of wire on each side of the straight portion of the shank, and a third strip bound on the side that will become the fly's belly. Obviously, this method works best on larger nymph hooks.

the pattern on a 1X-long, size 12 hook, tie an inverted version on a 2X-long, size 14 hook; the smaller bend and shorter point mean less weight that needs to be overbalanced.

After bending the hook, bind strips of weighting wire along the left and right sides of the shank, and then add a third piece of wire on the side that will become the fly's belly.

Cement the wraps with superglue. When it's fished on a floating line, a nymph tied on a bent, weighted hook will drift or swim with the point up.

An upside-down nymph's wing case goes on the same side of the hook shank as the bend and point. Otherwise, the fly is tied much like a conventional nymph. As you'd expect, this method of tying is easier on midsize and larger hooks than on small ones. Tying an upside-down nymph on a size 12, 2X-long frame isn't difficult; making one on a size 16 hook is more trouble than it's worth.

Besides trout patterns, tie some inverted nymphs for smallmouth bass. Bronzebacks love a big, black, shaggy nymph drifted right along the bottom. If you tie smallmouth nymphs upside down, you'll spend more time fishing and less replacing flies.

MONO WEED GUARDS

Flies tied on inverted hooks avoid many snags, but they can't dodge all of them. In some situations, a fly needs a guard or shield for the hook point. In drowned or fallen trees, for instance, a fly with a weed guard usually makes the most sense; even a Bend-Back can hang up in a tangle of submerged branches.

Wire weed guards have uses, but they also have drawbacks. They're tricky and time consuming to make. Your tippet can foul around a wire guard, rendering the fly useless until you fix the tangle. For all but the most extreme conditions, I prefer flies with monofilament weed guards.

The best weed guard I know is the style advocated by Ed Jaworowski, a great casting instructor and fly tier. Ed described this type of guard in an article for the Summer 1998 issue of *Fly Tyer* magazine. It looks pretty much like other mono weed guards: a piece of monofilament tied to the hook shank, bent around to the hook eye to form a loop, and secured behind the eye. But the way Ed attaches the mono at the rear of the hook makes his guard work better and last longer than other styles.

Most tiers bind a monofilament weed guard not just to the rear of the hook shank, but halfway down the bend. Then, after completing the fly, the tier brings the other end of the monofilament forward and attaches it to the front of the shank. That method does produce a protective loop of mono beneath the hook, but the loop doesn't retain its shape for long. As the fly bounces off obstructions, and particularly if it gets chomped by a fish, the mono bends where it exits the thread wraps holding it to the bend of the hook. The entire loop deforms and shifts rearward, exposing the hook point. After a couple of fish or a few hours of use, a fly with a guard made this way has no more snag resistance than a naked hook.

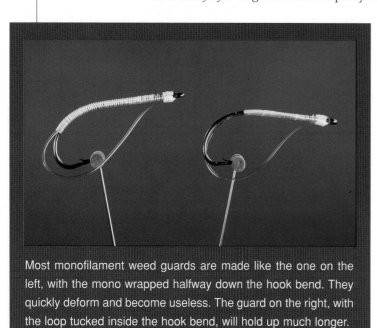

Most monofilament weed guards are made like the one on the left, with the mono wrapped halfway down the hook bend. They quickly deform and become useless. The guard on the right, with the loop tucked inside the hook bend, will hold up much longer.

Ed Jaworowski's method works much better. It produces a loop that protects the hook point, doesn't interfere with hooking a fish, and will not deform. It's easier to show than describe, so let's make one, using a big, bass-size bucktail as our example.

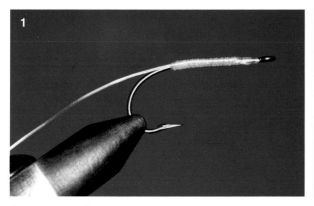

Cut a piece of monofilament about 6 inches long. Bind one end of the mono along the near side of the hook shank with two layers of thread. Do not wrap down into the bend. Cement the wraps with superglue.

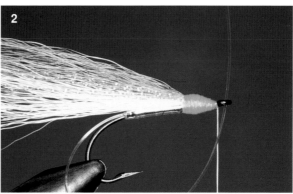

Tie the fly, in this case a simple green-over-white bucktail. After wrapping the fly's head, leave the thread hanging behind the hook eye. Bring the free end of the mono up through the eye.

Make two or three wraps of thread to bind the mono to the underside of the fly's nose. Don't make more than three wraps; you still need to adjust the size of the loop.

Remove the fly from the vise and tuck the loop of mono inside the hook bend. Adjust the loop to size (see the final two photos) by pulling on the end of the mono. Free the loop from the hook bend and put the fly back in the vise. Make a few more snug wraps of thread.

Bend the free end of the mono back and bind it down. This locks the material to the fly's head so that the weed guard cannot pull out.

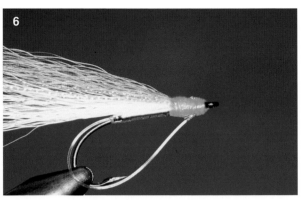

Clip the excess monofilament. Whip-finish the thread and cement the fly's head.

Tuck the loop inside the hook bend. Note the space between the guard and the point; this guard is the right length and shape for this hook. A weed guard made this way will not deform; when a fish bites, the loop moves to the side rather than to the rear. The guard will shield the hook point for as long as the fly stays in one piece.

Here's the fly with stick-on eyes and a coat of Softex on the head. The guard will resist virtually all snags, cannot foul the tippet, and will keep its shape through dozens of fish.

This type of weed guard works not only on warmwater and saltwater flies, but on some trout flies, too. If you want some weedless Muddlers, Woolly Buggers, and bucktails, tie them on 3X-long hooks and equip them with monofilament weed guards. (This type of guard doesn't work as well on longer hooks.) You can do the same thing with hellgrammites, big stoneflies, and damselfly nymphs tied on 3X-long hooks. With an assortment of snag-resistant flies, you will approach brush piles, sunken trees, and weed beds with a new attitude.

If it's too stiff, a weed guard can become a fish guard. Remember that a guard's function is to deflect the hook away from a snag, not to shove an obstruction out of the way. Monofilament guards don't need to be as heavy as some anglers think. For the type of guard shown above, I hardly ever use monofilament heavier than 20-pound test, even on a size 1/0 saltwater fly. On bass and pike flies, I generally use guards made with 15- to 20-pound leader material. If I need a stiffer guard—for casting to redfish in a spartina grass marsh, for instance—I might use 20-pound hard nylon such as that sold by Mason. I'd go heavier than that (maybe) only on a fly that I planned to slam into mangroves all day. But even there, I'd rather risk losing a few flies than missing a few strikes.

Weed guards on trout and smallmouth streamers are lighter. On a size 6 Muddler pattern, 10-pound mono is stiff enough; for fending off grass in a river, a guard made with 8-pound-test material will usually suffice.

Fluorocarbon is excellent weed-guard material. It's fairly stiff, very tough, and less visible than nylon. Fluorocarbon also weighs more than nylon, and a weed guard made with it can add some extra weight to a fly.

Weed guards and upside-down hooks can save money by reducing the number of flies you snag and have to break off. More important—much more important—they

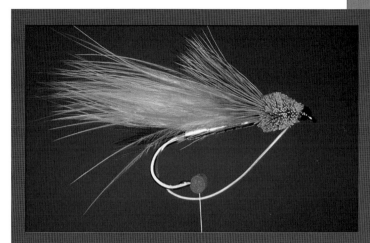

Weed guards aren't just for big saltwater, bass, and pike flies. A guard made of 10-pound-test leader material turns this size 6 Muddler into a more versatile and dangerous lure. The same type of guard works on big hellgrammite and stonefly patterns, too.

can make you a more effective angler. A fly fisher who attacks drowned timber, brush piles, weed beds, and riprap with confidence and even recklessness will catch more and bigger fish than an angler who timidly casts around the safe edges of hazards.

INDEX